Royal
Botanic Garden
Edinburgh

Scottish
PLANT
NAMES
An A to Z

Gregory J. Kenicer

Royal
Botanic Garden
Edinburgh

ISBN: 978-1-910877-44-9

© Royal Botanic Garden Edinburgh, 2023.
Published by the Royal Botanic Garden Edinburgh
20A Inverleith Row, Edinburgh, EH3 5LR
www.rbge.org.uk

Proceeds from sales of this book will be used to support the work of RBGE.

The Royal Botanic Garden Edinburgh is a Non Departmental Public Body (NDPB)
sponsored and supported through Grant-in-Aid by the
Scottish Government's Environment and Forestry Directorate (ENFOR).

The Royal Botanic Garden Edinburgh is a
Charity registered in Scotland (number SC007983).

Edited by
Frankie Mathieson and Sarah Worrall, Royal Botanic Garden Edinburgh
Design and layout by
Caroline Muir, Royal Botanic Garden Edinburgh
Printed by
McAllister Litho Glasgow Limited

9638549
Printed on Carbon Captured paper

Scottish
PLANT
NAMES
An A to Z

Gregory J. Kenicer

Illustrated by Hazel France

Contents

K O T
to to to
N S Z

| 131 | 165 | 219 |

Introduction

This book is about the names of plants in one small corner of the world and three languages in that small corner. As you dip into it, or refer to it for a name, you will spot clues as to how people have thought about plants in Scotland over the centuries. Some of the names are simply descriptive, others speak of the use of the plants, others are poetic or poignant. Some names have religious origins, or roots in wider folklore, while others are very recent inventions.

Names are incredibly powerful things. They are a crucial part of the way that we see and classify the world around us. This process of observing, classifying and naming is taxonomy – one of the oldest and most fundamental of scientific disciplines. Every human is a taxonomist; we instinctively group things, compare them and identify them, but it is only by giving these things a name that we can truly communicate them to others. The names hint at the many taxonomies that people have had for plants over the years, giving us an insight into their relationship with plants and ways of looking at the world.

Plant taxonomy is a major part of the work of the Royal Botanic Garden Edinburgh, and this book reflects that. *Scottish Plant Names: An A-Z* has its origins in the Garden's *Flora Celtica* project, which began collating Scottish plant names in the late 1990s and early 2000s. Established by William Milliken and Sam Bridgewater, the project's focus is on the plant lore of Scotland, and it is impossible to research plant uses without also recording the names being used for these plants. Contributions, made through subsequent years by Matt Elliot, Allan Elliott and a huge effort by Roger West, ultimately reached over 9,000 entries to the database of names. Given there are slightly over 1,000 species of flowering plants native to Scotland, this is a truly impressive total of names. Some of these are the standard English names used by the Botanical Society of Britain & Ireland – one name per species. A similar list of 'standard' Gaelic names was adopted by Pankhurst and Mullin for their *Flora of the Outer Hebrides* (1991), covering mostly the plants from the islands, although some other standard names have been designated in the Gaelic lexicon since. Even taking this into account, that is only around

2,000 standard common names. The remaining 7,000 reflect the richness of Scotland's languages and the importance of plants to its people through the ages.

The World Flora Online project, includes the full database of plant names in both Scots and Gaelic and can be found here: worldfloraonline.org

LANGUAGE IN SCOTLAND

Scotland's rich linguistic history is as varied as its flora; from the almost completely forgotten Pictish language to the dozens of global languages spoken today. This book delves into the botany of these languages, and although the focus is very much on the three major living 'native languages', **Gaelic, English and Scots**, the influences of many other tongues can be seen throughout. These influences reflect a mixture of isolation, innovation, movements and contacts with other peoples, borrowings, mishearings and the slow evolution of words. It is only in relatively recent years that the Pictish language, which is known only from a few names of people and places, has been recognised as a Brythonic (British) P-Celtic language. Pictish was largely supplanted by the Goidelic (Gaelic) Q-Celtic language from the 5th century onwards as invasion and settlement from Ireland established the kingdom of Dál Riata. Shortly after this, the Anglian influence and invasions from the south, and later still, the Norse languages from the north were introduced as a consequence of yet more invasion and settlement. The confluence of these two latter languages gave rise to various facets of the Scots language – the Norse element still strongly evident in the northern and Doric Scots dialects. In turn, the Anglian language and later courtly French gave rise to English as we know it today. As the adoption of French words show, diplomacy and equally trade were major influences too – it's certainly not all about invasions!

Language is a very dynamic thing and each of these major Scottish languages has the typical array of regional dialects and even very localised quirks that one expects to find in any language that has been around for a long time. Many completely novel words arise all the time, and while it is easier for them to travel in today's globalised, instantly connected society, we can see similarly original words appear throughout history. Plant names are a great example, with children's games as one of the richest sources, so we see the long stalks of rosebay willowherb (*Chamerion angustifolium*), stripped of their leaves thrown, and known, as 'javelins', or the edible centre of thistle-heads called 'cheesies' after the texture of this popular impromptu snack – sort of a budget artichoke heart.

PLANT NAMES

Formal, scientific taxonomy uses binomials: two-part names that consist of a genus and specific epithet. Humans are, of course, *Homo sapiens*, while the bitter vetch, or heath pea, is known as *Lathyrus linifolius*, a lovely little blue and pink-flowered member of the pea family found in heaths and acid grasslands. Traditionally, this plant was dug up and the small tubers on the rhizomes were chewed to alleviate hunger and supposedly provide a boost of energy.

Lathyrus is the genus name. There are over 140 species of *Lathyrus* worldwide, including the more famous sweet pea (*L. odoratus*).

Linifolius is the specific epithet – in this case describing the often slender (linear) leaflets of this species.

In some texts, you will find the name, or names, of the researchers who first described the species in this Western scientific tradition – in this case, the German botanists Reichard and Bässler.

'Bitter vetch' is closely related to the true vetches, but lives in open heath and grassland, so lacks tendrils on the leaves for climbing that are commonly found on other vetches. It's also not really that bitter to chew – it has more of a sweet anise-flavour (although we would not recommend trying it)! In fact, it was often used as a 'liquorice' to flavour whisky and other strong spirits. It may be that it is bitter in the same sense as many botanicals used to flavour booze are known as bitters. To compound the confusion, several other plants are known as 'bitter vetch' in English, including *Vicia orobus*, the wood bitter vetch, and some other members of the genera *Vicia* and *Ervilia*. Most of our records of the plant being used in recent centuries are from Gaelic-speaking areas, so it has accrued a large number of Gaelic names, as well as many in Scots – in fact,

this species alone has over 25 names across the three languages in Scotland. Several of the Scots names are evidently derived from the Gaelic *cairmeal*, which becomes 'carmylie' in Scots. In Gaelic, the name is interpreted as 'dig and enjoy', or 'meal from the moss/heath', but it loses this meaning in Scots, and just becomes a name for the plant – albeit hinting perhaps coincidentally at caramel. With all these names floating about for one humble little plant in Scotland alone, the number of names it must have across the parts of Europe where it is found probably run to over 100. This is one of the reasons botanists use these standard 'Latin' taxonomic names. For this book, however, we articulate the names around the most common 'official' English name as that is likely more familiar to the reader. You can still find out the taxonomic name in the main entries for each species.

The large number of names for bitter vetch is fairly typical for such a useful, attractive and easily identifiable plant. In contrast unassuming little sedges, such as *Carex spicata* have only a single English (spiked sedge) and Gaelic name (*seisg spìceach*). In this case, the Latin, English and Gaelic all mean the same thing, as the English and Gaelic are simply direct translations from the scientific Latin name.

ORIGINS OF NAMES

The origins of plant names are hugely varied. Many simply describe the plant's appearance, such as *cnapan dubh*, 'the black knob', referring to the dense, dark, knobbly flowerheads of the lesser knapweed (*Centaurea nigra*). Others take a variant, misspelling or mishearing of a descriptive name and end up creating something new – 'meal and folie' is a Scots name for yarrow (*Achillea millefolium*), derived from the French 'millefeuille', which means 'thousand leaves', describing the intricately divided, lacy leaf. This is taken even further in more recent Anglicised Scots to become the name 'melancholy'. This is a somewhat strange concept for such a cheerful plant that was used as a vulnerary (a traditional herbal medicine) to help cure wounds. Without awareness of the derivation of the name it might be easy to develop a whole story about how yarrow might have been considered a 'melancholy' plant – perhaps a plant to treat melancholy. Perhaps the plant was melancholy as it was unable to save the life of the Greek hero Achilles after he was hit by the Trojan Paris's poisoned arrow. Achilles, who gives his name to the taxonomic name of the plant, had been taught how to heal with it by Chiron, his centaur guardian. We should emphasise this connection to melancholy is not something we have come across in research – I just made it up, but it is exactly the kind of pattern we see in the ways that folklore and names interweave. This evolution of plant names and their meanings is delightfully rich, and it is easy to see how it ties intricately with folklore, prompting numerous original folk ideas as the language evolves.

Origins – Animals and Plants

Many names derive from a plant's similarity to other plants, so we have the aquatic *Menyanthes trifoliata* as bogbean in English – the thick, slightly grey-green trefoil leaves (leaves made up of three leaflets) are reminiscent of the leaves of the broad bean, while the fruit itself is somewhat like a bean. Of course, some such names are quite poetically tongue-in-cheek, so the humble little duckweed (*Lemna* species), which is essentially a miniscule floating leaf/stem structure with perhaps the smallest flower of any plant, is sometimes known in Gaelic as *ros lachan* – 'the duck's rose'.

Birds and other animals regularly appear in names – usually as a shorthand for particular properties of the plant. 'Dog' can refer to a cruder, less-refined version of a species, or to a low-growing habit, perhaps hinting that dogs would urinate on it in preference to the larger version – so silverweed (*Argentina anserina*) becomes 'dog's tansy' – the leaf is superficially similar to that of tansy (*Tanacetum vulgare*), but the plant is a shorter, creeping pathside and coastal species. Incidentally, this same species is also known under the English names 'goose grass' and 'swine's grass', with geese foraging among the coastal grasslands in which it grows, and pigs digging the plants up to eat the starchy roots. Inevitably, fodder for livestock is a theme that appears quite often – perhaps more in English and Scots than Gaelic. This extends to seaweeds such as the channelled wrack (*Pelvetia canaliculata*) known as 'calf-weed', or 'cow tang'

in Orkney, for its use in fattening cattle for market. In a related vein, some plants were believed to cause illness in livestock and acquired names like 'cow-cracker' (*Silene vulgaris* – the bladder campion), or 'sheep root' (*Pinguicula vulgaris* – the butterwort). This latter species was unfairly blamed for rotting the feet of sheep that ate it. But it grows in wet habitats, and if you graze your sheep in a bog, what do you expect to happen? This explanation might be a bit unfair though, as the name acts as a shorthand to identify boggy ground, as *Pinguicula* is a great indicator species for such habitats. Some plants *are* truly dangerous to livestock, with ragwort (*Senecio jacobaea*) particularly notorious, although incidents of poisoning are rare. It is generally avoided by cattle and horses, as it has a bitter taste, so it can appear to take over in fields. If it is eaten, though, the unfortunate animals can suffer stomach lesions and death as the array of toxic alkaloids break down, causing liver failure – perhaps reinforcing its name of 'stinking weed' even though it does have a slightly sickly sweet scent. Ragwort is also one of several plants called 'witches' steed' in English and in Scots it was 'wee-bo' (a euphemism for the Devil). Again, these are possible reflections of its evil reputation, although it was also part of the traditional medicine chest, an alternative to willow for creel making and as a 'switch for cows, horses and children' (Carmichael, 1928). Ragwort's close relative, *Senecio vulgaris*, fares little-better in the naming stakes.

It is considered such a vigorous weed, it is known as groundsel in English – a somewhat cryptic name until we look at the Scots 'grunny swally', or 'Doric gruniswallow' – the swallower of ground.

Some of the most interesting names are, of course, 'just the name for that plant'. In some cases, these are truly ancient names that can be tracked through to their earliest Indo-European origins. Names such as *beithe* (Gaelic) and birch (English), both of which refer to the birches (*Betula*), tie back to similar names throughout Europe's history and prehistory for the iconic, white-barked tree with superbly useful wood and bark. Trees are unsurprisingly the plants with the most ancient names, so we see the Gaelic *seileach*, Scots 'sauch' and English sallow as names for the most versatile willows. Their Latin-derived taxonomic name is *Salix*.

Naming for similarity can extend to almost anything, so the slender, curving stems of bramble (*Rubus fruticosus*) are one of several plants called 'Leddy's garters' in Scots, or lady's garters in English. One can't help thinking there is perhaps more to this name than meets the eye, though, as these particular 'garters' would be made from coarse, thorny material rather than silk and lace.

Political and Social Names
More obviously scurrilous names appear as well, with sectarian or political undertones common for plants with an unpleasant smell. Thus, there are several plants called 'Stinking Billy' in honour of William of Orange. 'Carl-Doddies' – a name for ribwort plantain (*Plantago*

lanceolata) is a relatively balanced example – the 'Charles' and 'George' of the name represent the Jacobean and Hanoverian dynasties. These common grassland and lawn plants are used in a fighting game. The long stalked flowerheads are whipped against each other, taking turns until one or other of the monarchs loses their head. Children's games and snacks are a great source of plant names, but almost any useful plant inevitably picks up many names – whether they are edible, medicinal or used in construction. On the more romantic side, the *shidhe*, or faerie folk and other aspects of magic and witchcraft are major sources of names as well, so in Gaelic many plants relate to the 'Ban-sidh', or 'Ban-sith', the faerie woman whose name appears as the banshee of Irish folklore.

As can be seen, the diversity and evolution of names is intricate and fascinating. We have picked out some further examples of these themes and patterns throughout this book as little snippets scattered through the text, but you will doubtlessly spot many more connections and patterns as you dip into the text. Part of the fun is interpreting these connections for yourself, although really delving into the etymology and uncovering the story of a name can be a big job, and of course many stories of names, their meanings and links are lost to time.

Orthographic Variants

A great many plants are named for variations on an existing name, a phenomenon seen across each of the languages we consider in this book. Particularly interesting are those names that appear to have adopted new meanings as these orthographic variants slight changes in spelling can suggest a completely new interpretation. In many cases, however, reliable testament to the uses of the names with these new meanings is a bit patchy. Some may have been recorded wrongly when transcribed from what the author heard onto the page, but standardisations of spellings are a relatively recent thing, especially in Gaelic and Scots, so many of these orthographic variants were legitimately recorded. It is likely that many variant spellings had their new meaning attached after the event, the misspelling then being back-translated by a writer in the absence of speakers to give the original intended meaning. Recording was seldom done completely systematically.

But to be fair, language is anything but systematic as it evolves. For those words used mostly in an oral tradition, we can seldom be certain of their exact histories. A nice example of this array of allied names with many meanings comes from *Silene dioica* – red campion:

- *Cìrean choilich*, *cìrean choileach* and *cìrean coilich* are all translated as 'cockscomb' – nicely suggestive of the lobed pinkish-red petals
- *Coirean coilich* as 'the little cock's cauldron'
- *Coirean coilleach* suggests a meeting in a woodland – appropriate for this species' habitat, although *coirean* is the general name adopted for the campions, so we have the Botanical Society of Britain & Ireland (BSBI) standard accepted Gaelic name for *Silene uniflora* (sea campion) as *Coirean na mara*

It is important to note that these translations are taken directly from the source material in each case. We have not attempted to 'clean up' or rationalise any names, so some translations may seem strange to modern readers, but this is part of the richness of these languages, and it presents an excellent opportunity to see the myriad ways in which our relationship with plants and their names evolves. John Cameron's treasure trove, *Gaelic Names of Plants* (1883), gives extensive etymologies along with many fascinating snippets of wider lore. He says of the field mushroom (*Agaricus campestris* or *A. bisporus*) that:

'*Balg bhuachail* (balg is an ancient Celtic word, and in

most languages has the same signification—viz., a bag, wallet, pock, &:c. (Greek, (βολγυς; Latin, *bulga*; Sax. *beige*; Ger. *balg, buachail*, a shepherd). *Balg losgainn* (*losgann* a frog, and in some places *bàlg bhuachair— buacar* = dung).'

This provides a wonderful explanation for how the Gaelic name *Balg bhuchail* might equally mean 'frog's bag' or 'dung-bag'. Indeed, these mushrooms typically grow in moist fields and pastures enriched with animal dung, excellent habitats for frogs. Furthermore, Cameron usually tries to demonstrate the similarities and distinctions between Scottish and Irish Gaelic, and his work is understandably considered the go-to source for Gaelic plant names.

Sources and Standard Names

The vast majority of the entries in this account have been drawn from existing publications, and there is a wealth of these studies through the past 150 years or so, but there is an even longer history of recording what was happening in rural Scotland. The plants people were using in their everyday lives, for example, appear in crown edicts, poetry and treatises on witchcraft and medicine through the ages. We are extremely fortunate that people like the renowned Martin Martin were recording aspects of the oral tradition, including names of plants. Martin was a physician, trained under Robert Sibbald, co-founder of the Royal Botanic Garden Edinburgh, Royal College of Physicians of Edinburgh *and* the Geographer Royal for Scotland.

One of Sibbald's projects was to inventorise the 'natural products' of Scotland, and to that end, he commissioned Martin to travel in the 1690s to the Gaelic-speaking areas of the country – particularly in the west – and record the geography, customs, archaeology and ethnobotany of the people there. As a native Gaelic speaker, Martin had a particular opportunity to record the oral tradition first-hand, and as such his work is invaluable for our understanding of the culture at the time. Also, being a physician, he was well-trained in the use and identification of plants, so we can be confident of many of his identifications. Slightly later, poets such as Duncan Ban MacIntyre (Donnchadh Bàn Mac an t-Saoir), writing in the 18th century, employed a fairly standard set of names for common plants, and it is most of these that have become the Gaelic 'standard' names. Their use was widespread, and in the same way as the standard English names, they were the ones that found their way into dictionaries. Many countries identify standard common names for each botanical species in the main or official languages of the country, so in both Turkey and Japan, for example, a botanist describing a plant species as new to science will suggest a new 'official' name in Turkish or Japanese respectively. From a botanical standpoint in Scotland, many Gaelic 'standard' names were proposed by Pankhurst and Mullin (1991), while the BSBI maintains the English language list. Of the 70 or so different species of grass-like *Carex* (sedges) in Britain, for example, only a very few would have been recognised as distinct – usually on the basis of particularly striking characters or usefulness. The rest would be lumped under 'sedge', which is also a term for the kind of dense, wet grassy vegetation between a pasture and a swamp that many species of *Carex* favour.

The work of lexicographers John Jamieson (1808) for Scots and Edward Dwelly (1920 and later editions) for Gaelic are the best-known dictionaries for the respective languages, distilling many sources together into dedicated dictionaries. However, Dwelly's Gaelic dictionary had several botany-specific lexicographies to draw on with the work of Cameron (1883), of particular value. Writing almost a century after Jamieson,

John Wood's 1891 paper for the Andersonian Naturalists' Society (1893) is an interesting tract that adds many names in Scots, as well as delivering a pithy explanation for Jamieson's apparent bias towards the agricultural:

'In [Jamieson's] Dictionary the only plants which have attracted a fair share of notice are the grasses, the plants which occur as troublesome weeds in cultivated ground, those which are sought after for their real or supposed medicinal virtues, and those which produce edible fruits. There is no attempt made at classification, for botanical knowledge was in its initial empiric stage. The same name is often applied to plants of totally different classes, or the name of one plant is applied to the whole family. The names are for the most part of Anglo-Saxon origin, but, as might have been expected, we have many names derived from Gaelic and French sources.

To proceed then, let us take first the grasses.'

It is only in relatively recent times that standardisation of spelling has been imposed on language, so in Gaelic, English and Scots we are very lucky that many writers saw fit to include regional and orthographic (spelling) variants in their works. This gives us important insights into local linguistic quirks, as well as the vagaries and potential pitfalls of capturing the oral tradition.

We have chosen to retain as many of these variations as possible, through the diligent work of Roger West in particular. Following the tradition of most botanical dictionaries, we have tried to indicate the areas where names were used or the regional dialects to which they belong. More recent oral history finds its way into this publication through the work of people such as the Highland journalist Mary Beith, herbalist Anne Barker and former colleagues at the Royal Botanic Garden Edinburgh, William Milliken and Sam Bridgewater, who developed and ran the *Flora Celtica* project.

A recent work by the artist Derek Robertson, entitled *Bho Bheul an Eòin / From the Bird's Mouth,* drew in a consortium of Gaelic speakers and natural historians to identify new names for dozens of species only recently recognised in Scotland, in many cases those that have moved here as a consequence of climate change. This beautifully represents the responsiveness of language to an ever-changing natural world.

As a final note, the exhaustively researched and referenced resources provided by groups such as Sabhal Mòr Ostaig, the Scots Language Society and Scottish National Dictionary Association are invaluable and go to show quite how vibrant these languages are. For a deeper and more detailed delve into the breadth of sources we cannot recommend them enough.

HOW TO USE THIS BOOK

This book is not a complete dictionary of plant names but pulls out many of the most common and familiar plants as well as those with the richest seams of names. It also includes algae, fungi and a few lichens as well – as is fitting for the broad church of a botanic garden. We have chosen to articulate the entries around the 'official' common English name, given the majority of the readership are likely to have some degree of fluency in English and these common names are often the most familiar. The temptation for a botanist to articulate everything around esoteric taxonomic (Latin) names has been resisted, but we have included these throughout for reference.

Most of the names have been taken directly from secondary sources. Where explanations of the names are given, these are also taken from the secondary sources, so we make no claims for their veracity, and indeed that is part of the point— that the people using or recording the names may have different interpretations of the meanings. So please do not get too furious at what appears to be our misinterpretation of meanings. The core sources are listed below, but entries are not specifically referenced by source. Our underlying database contains this information and is available to consult. The database was hugely edited down for this publication, with many 'minor names' and duplicates as well as most agricultural, ecological and plant anatomy phrases removed for reasons of space.

Poetry and other literature contain many references to one or a few plants. Although the great majority of these have been collated in existing works on plant names, and thereby found their way into this book, a few variant spellings are seemingly not recorded. For example, James Hogg's (1770–1835) protagonist in *The Witch of Fife* rides to the Sabbat on a 'humloke schaw' (hemlock stalk) saddled with a 'moon fern leaf' – the humloke spelling is known from here, but not otherwise recorded in our main sources (albeit many similar spellings are). Some names were collected first-hand as part of the *Flora Celtica* project and informal interviews and chats, and these are used with permission.

The final caveat is that areas of overlap between formal Scots and informal Scottish-English are fluid, so some of the entries under Scots could be argued to be English and vice versa, and we apologise in advance if we upset anyone in categorising the names.

Gaelic alphabet of tree names

The 18 letters of the Gaelic alphabet are traditionally tied into the identities of trees and shrubs – partly as a mnemonic to help remember the letters. Some plants appear twice, and there is a bit of disagreement over a few of them, but a common working list is something like this:

AILM – Elm (*Ulmus glabra*)

BEITH – Birch (*Betula* species)

COLL – Hazel (*Corylus avellana*)

DAIR – Oak (*Quercus* species)

EADHA – Aspen (*Populus tremula*)

FÈARN – Alder (*Alnus glutinosa*)

GORT – Ivy (*Hedera helix*)

IOGH – Yew (*Taxus baccata*)

LUIS – Rowan (*Sorbus aucuparia*)

MUIN – Vine or bramble
(*Vitis* species or *Rubus fruticosus*)

NUIN – Ash (*Fraxinus excelsior*)

OIR / ONN – Gorse (*Ulex* species)

PEITH BHOG – Downy birch
(Betula *pubescens*) – the soft P
sound is often linked to this tree,
although the name is seldom if ever
uscd for the tree

RUIS – Elder

SUIL – Willow

TEINE – Gorse (*Ulex* species)

UATH – Hawthorn
(*Crataegus monogyna*)

UR – Heather – albeit an obscure
and local use of the word

A
to
E

A

ADDER'S TONGUE
(*Ophioglossum vulgatum*)

ENGLISH: Cock's comb

GAELIC: *Beasan* (W Highlands); *Feasan*; *Gath na nathrach*; *Lus na nathrach*/*Lus na nathraith* – snake/serpent's weed/plant; *Teanga a' nathrach*/*Teanga na nathrach* – adder's tongue

Adder's tongue, and many of the names in Gaelic, describes the slender fertile frond emerging from the broad green main frond of this little grassland fern. It is certainly reminiscent of a serpent's flickering tongue, so was used to treat snakebites, although the victim was probably just as likely to survive without using the so-called 'adder's spear' ointment.

AGRIMONY
(*Agrimonia eupatorium*)

GAELIC: *Geurach* – the sharp bitter one; *A geurag-bhileach* – acid-leaved; *Geur-bhileach* – green, sharp, sour-leaved, perhaps because of the serrated leaves and/or sharp taste; *Mirean* – the frolicsome one; *Mirean nam magh* – merry one in the field; *Muir-dhroighinn* – piercing suffering; *Mur-druidhean*: *Mur* = sorrow and *druid* = druid/magician, so a cure for various sorrows or illnesses

Common agrimony has a sharp taste sometimes likened to apricot and was used widely across Europe medicinally. Some uses included being ingested/worn to protect against bullets in the Renaissance or to cure insomnia when placed under the sleeper's head. It is relatively rare in Scotland but was probably once cultivated widely and was a standard part of the apothecary's stock from mediaeval times.

ALDER
(*Alnus glutinosa*)

ENGLISH: Scotch mahogany – of the rich dense red wood as a timber

GAELIC: *Crann-feàrna*; *Craobh-feàrna*: *Craobh* = tree; *Droimlein*; *Drumanach*; **Feàrn**; *Am feàrna*; *Ruaim*

SCOTS: Aar; Aller; Allertree; Alrone – this name is archaic; Arn

This distinctive waterside tree's names are mostly ancient, reflecting its value as a water-resistant timber since prehistoric times. **Feàrn represents the letter F in the Gaelic alphabet of trees.**

ALEXANDERS
(*Smyrnium olusatrum*)

GAELIC: *Lus nan gran dubh* – the plant with black seeds

SCOTS: Alishunners; Alshinder; Alshinders

This stately and vigorous (i.e. kind of weedy) member of the carrot family is common in warm spots in central Scotland – often near disturbed ground. An escapee from cultivation in monasteries and other medicinal gardens, the black fruits were used as a spice and the leaves were a common pot-herb.

ALMOND
(*Prunus dulcis*)

GAELIC: *Almon*; *Cno almoin* – almond nut; *Cno ghreugach* – Greek nut; *Craobh almoin* – almond tree; *A mon*

SCOTS: Mand or mane – in a possible interpretation of almond cakes or bread

Almond is not native to Scotland, although it has been grown here in warmer late-mediaeval times (and may well be again as the climate warms). However, it has garnered a range of Gaelic names largely based around the English name.

ANGELICA, WILD
(*Angelica sylvestris*)

GAELIC: *Aingealag*; *Bun an iuran*; *Contran*; *Cuinneag-mhighe* – whey-bucket; *Galluran* – perhaps from gall, milk; *Geobhastan*; *Gleorann*; *Iuran*; *Lus an lonaidh* – churn-handle plant; *Lus nam buadh / Lus nam buadha* – plant of virtue or power; *Meacan-righ-fiadhain* – wild king's-root

SCOTS: Ait skeiter / Ait skeeter (Morayshire and elsewhere); Skytes, Spoots (Shetland); Switiks (Shetland)

Like several of the large umbellifers (members of the carrot family), wild angelica has a hollow stem – ideal for making a pea-shooter, or as the Scots names suggest, an oat-shooter. It was also used to curdle milk – hence its associations with churn-staves and other links to dairy.

APPLE
(*Malus* species and cultivars)

ENGLISH: Crab; Crab apple

GAELIC: *Abhal*

SCOTS: Aiple / Aipple / Apill / Aple / Appil / Eipple; Craw aipple / Craw's aipple – Crow's apple; Oslin; Pome; Scrab (Berwickshire / Roxburghshire); Scribe; Scrog / Scrogg; Scrubby; Yap

Although this list looks long, most of the names are variants. The 'apple'-sounding ones referring to all apples, including cultivated dessert and cooking varieties, while the other names usually refer to the wild crab apples or similar small, sharp, cultivated varieties.

ASH
(*Fraxinus excelsior*)

GAELIC: *Crann-uinnsinn; Craobh uinnseann; Craobh uinnsinn; Crobh uinnseann; Fuinnseann; Nuin; Oinsean; Oinseann; Uinnse; Uinnseann; Uinsinn*

SCOTS: Esch / Esche; Eschis; Esh

Ash is an extremely important tree across European tradition, so ash, esh and *uinnse* all share the same ancient root with the Latin '*ornus*'. The Gaelic names mostly imply that the timber is particularly durable. **Nuin represents the letter N in the Gaelic alphabet of trees.**

ASPEN
(*Populus tremula*)

GAELIC: *A' chritheann; Crann-crithinn / Craobh-chrithinn* – trembling tree; *An critheach; An critheann* – the trembler; *Crithran eadha; Eabh* – Eve (wife of Adam); *Eadha; Eadhadh* – smarting; *Eagh* – trembling; *Eibheadh*

ENGLISH/SCOTS: Esp; Old wives' tongues; Quakin aish; Quakin ash; Tremlin tree

Most of these names relate to the leaves of aspen, which tremble and whisper in the slightest breeze. Several traditions suggest the leaves never rest out of some perceived guilt – this is one of many trees where the wood was supposedly used to make the crucifix, although the English/Scots 'old wives' tongues' has a more earthy and cheeky meaning. **Eadha represents the letter E in the Gaelic alphabet of trees.**

B

BARBERRY
(*Berberis vulgaris*)

GAELIC: *Barbrag* – brilliancy of a shell; *Bragaire* (Lewis); *Gearr-dhearc*; *Gearr-dhearcag*; *Preas deilgneach* – prickly bush; *Preas nan gear dhearc / Preas-nan-geur-dhearc* – sour-berry bush; *Treabhach*

SCOTS: Barruba; Berber; Guild (Fife, Perthshire and Selkirkshire); Gule tree – an archaic term

Barberry is a hedgerow shrub that is not common in Scotland, and it is difficult to tell if it was brought in by humans or is a native part of the flora. In any case, it has garnered many names as it is distinctive and useful – the tart edible berries were used as an early gastric medicine to treat stomach complaints and as a flavouring for food.

BARLEY
(*Hordeum* species)

GAELIC: *Eàrna*; *Eòrna*; *Eòrnan* – is a diminutive applied to the two-rowed barley (*Hordeum distichon*)

SCOTS: Ann – of the bristle-like awns, Barleke; Barley grain – of the fruit; Barley pickle; Barlie; Bigg – a particular variety; Chester barley/Chester bere (Angus) – a particular variety; Ware barley (mostly northern) – barley manured with seaweed; Bair / Bar / Bear / Bere all apply to the six- or four-rowed barleys

A fairly consistent set of names for one of the most important crops in Scotland, the source of barley breads, beers and, of course, whisky. The wider language around particular cultivated varieties and the parts of the barley plant is extensive and worthy of a book in itself!

BAY LAUREL
(*Laurus nobilis*)

GAELIC: *Casgair* – slaughter, hit out; *Crann-cosgair* – tree of slaughter, from *cosgair* = 'queller or pacifier'; *Crann-laoibhreil* (or *cran*) tree with rich foliage/laurel/bay tree; *Craobh-chosgair*; *Craobh-laibhreis* – laurel tree; *Labhras*; *Laibhreal*; *Laibhreas* – tree with richness of foliage; *Ur uaine* – green bay tree

SCOTS: Lary; Laurean; Lawranel; Lorer, including a laurel arbor or grove

Another tree with an ancient name. In English, Scots and Gaelic, as well as Latin (*Laurus*) the name derives from the same root. Admittedly, several of the writers trace it back to different roots, drawing parallels with the Sanskrit words uih 'of the palm', labh to 'take or desire' and labhasa 'abundance of foliage'.

In Gaelic, however, the name *casgair* is unrelated, but is said to imply its association with battle, victory and the ensuing peace.

BEAN
(*Vicia faba* and *Phaseolus* species)

GAELIC: *Ponair* – bean; *Ponair airneach* – kidney bean; *Ponair Fhrangach* – French bean; *Ponair nan each* – horse bean (*Vicia faba*)

SCOTS: Bane; Bene; Swap; Whaup

Broad bean is *Vicia faba*; *Phaseolus* are the French and climbing beans.

BEARBERRY
(*Arctostaphylos uva-ursi*)

GAELIC: *Braoileag* – berry (Colonsay); *Braoileag-nan-con* – dog's berry; *Goirt-dhearc* – sour red: *Goirt* = sour and *dearg* = red; *Grainnseag* – grain-like berry; *Lus-na-geire-boireannach* – female plant of sharpness from *geire* = sharpness and *boireannach* = female; *Lusra na geire-boirnigh* – plant of bitterness: *Geire* = bitterness and *boirnigh* = feminine

SCOTS: Brawlins, braw = bear (N Scotland); Brylies; Craneberry-wire (Ross); Creashak (Rosshire); Dogberry (Aberdeenshire); Gnashaks (Banffshire and Moray); Gnashick (Banffshire and Moray); Nashag (Caithiness); Rapperdandie; Rapperdandy (Berwickshire and elsewhere)

Bearberry and cowberry (*Vaccinium vitis-idaea*) are similar plants, so some of the Scots names are seemingly shared between the two. Both produce small red berries, although those on bearberry are smaller and more tart, which is perhaps why many of the Gaelic names pick up on this to aid identification in the field. Bearberry is sharp or sour (goirt) and small like a grain, or 'female' relative to the larger 'male' fruits of the cowberry.

BEECH
(*Fagus sylvatica*)

GAELIC: *Beith na measathe* – fruiting birch; *Crann-faidhbhile* – beech tree; *Craobh fhaidhbhile*, perhaps; *Faibhile*; *Faidhbhile*; *Oruin*

SCOTS: Buck

Most of these names for beech are simply the name for the plant. There is some suggestion that *faidhbhile* derives from the same as the Greek 'fagos' – the name for the same tree. The copper beech (*Fagus sylvatica* 'Atropurpurea') is *faibhile dubh* or *faidhbhile dubh*, 'the black beech', which is a nice interpretation of the deep-purple leaves.

BENT
(*Agrostis* species of grasses)

ENGLISH: Bents, Bread and cheese

GAELIC: *Muirineach* – possibly 'ocean's bounty' or 'ocean's generosity'; *Muran*; *Fioran dubh* is black bent (*A. gigantea*)

SCOTS: Blaw-grass

Like many grasses important in agriculture, the bents have picked up several distinctive names, with most applied across several similar species.

BETONY
(*Betonica officinalis*)

ENGLISH: Maskwort

GAELIC: *Biatas* – the plant that maintains and nourishes, from *biadh* = food; *Glasair-coille* – the green one of the wood; *Lus beathaig* – life plant, nourishing plant; *Lusan-ceann-oir-a'-sgadan* – the little herb of the Herring's golden head (Sutherland); *Lus-beathaig* – Rebecca's plant: *Beathag* = Rebecca, *Lus-mhic-beathag*, *Lus mhic beathag*, or possibly *beathaig*

The green leaves were used as both salad and a tea substitute, but it is interesting to see the Old Testament's Rebecca being woven into the name as well. The Sutherland name alluding to the Herring's golden head is intriguing, and one for the Gaelic scholars.

BILBERRY/BLAEBERRY
(*Vaccinium myrtillus*)

ENGLISH: Wild blueberry; Whortleberry

GAELIC: *Caora bhidheag* (South Uist, Eriskay); *Caora-bhiodagan* (South Uist, Eriskay); *Caora-mhitheag*; *Cnaimhseag*; *Coaramh theag* (Skye, Dunkeld, Talmine); *Corra mheagan*; *Craoiseag* – from craos = a wide mouth (Lochaber); *Curach mheig* (Bernera Skye); *Dearc bhraoileag*; *Dearca-coille* – woodland berry (Colonsay); *Dearcag-dubh*; *Dearcag-mhonaidh* – mountain berry (Lochaber); *Dearcan-fithich* / *Dearchan-fithich* – raven's berries; *Dearc-fhraoich* / *Dearcan fhraoich* / *Dearc-an-fraoich* – berry of the heather; *Dearc roide* / *Dearc-an-roide* – wormwood/bitter/gall berry; *Fiadhag* / *Fiagag* (Sutherland); *Fraoch a bhidh*; *Fraoch nan curra-bhitheag*; *Fraochag*; *Fraochan* – [i.e. berries] growing among the heather; *Gearr-dhearc* / *Geur-dhearc* – sour berry; *Lus nan braoileag* / *Lus nan dearc* – the berry plant

SCOTS: Blaeberry, Blairdie (NE Scotland); Blivert (Aberdeenshire)

Phew! This extensive list of names will by no means be comprehensive, as the easy identification, delicious flavour and wide distribution mean the blaeberry will have picked up many local names now lost to time. The fabled blaeberry is known to this day as a tasty impromptu snack when out hiking (assuming not too many dogs are around)!

BINDWEED
(*Calystegia* and *Convolvulus* species)

SCOTS: Binwuid; Creepin eevie (NE Scotland)

BIRCHES
(*Betula pubescens* and *B. pendula*)

GAELIC: *Beatha*; **Beith**; *Beith charraigeach* – knotty or warty of *B. pendula*; *Beatha cluasach*; *Beithe dhubh-chasach* – dark-footed birch; *Beithe-dhubh* – black birch of *B. pendula*

SCOTS: Birk; Birken tree; Birkin; Birks

The relatively few names for birch seem to go against the grain (if you pardon the pun), that useful plants garner many names. In this case, we have a plant so universally known, useful and identifiable that it really only has one name with orthographic tweaks. Indeed, it is a similar name across most Indo-European languages. The two species of birch trees are not usually distinguished in the Scottish languages and the shrubby dwarf birch, *Betula nana,* is a relatively uncommon plant, usually from montane areas, so has picked up only the intuitive *beatha-beag* – 'small birch'. **Beith represents the letter B in the Gaelic alphabet of tree names.** The letter P is the soft P sound represented by *peith bhog*, a name associated with downy birch (*B. pubescens*).

BIRCH POLYPORE
(*Piptoporus betulinus*)

ENGLISH: Razor strop fungus; Soft tinder; Touchwood

GAELIC: *Cailleach spuigne* – soft, cheese-like sponge, from Irish Gaelic, and corrupted to more literally mean 'old woman sponge'

This bracket fungus was the source of 'amadou' tinder – dried and flaked then mixed with saltpetre (potassium nitrate) or other flammable agents. It was also the main fungus used for honing an edge on a razor.

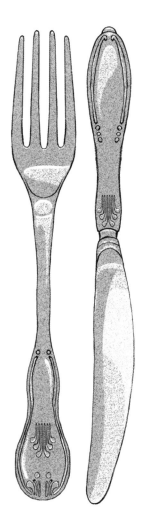

BIRDSFOOT TREFOIL
(*Lotus corniculatus*)

ENGLISH: Cat's claws; Deervetch; Eggs and bacon; Shamrock

GAELIC: *Adharc an diabhaill* – Devil's horns; *Bar a-mhìslean / Barra-mhìslean* – flower that springs; *Blàthan-buidhe-nam-bo* – yellow bloom of the cow; *Cnuadhan a' chait*; *Eala bhuidhe*; *Maide-millis*; *Peasair a' Mhadaidh-ruadh* (Fox's peas)

SCOTS: Bloom-fell; Catcluke; Catten clover; Cockies an'hennies; Craw's taes; Craw-taes; Horse Yakkels (Shetland); Kattaklu / Katt-kler (Shetland); Knives and forks

This common little plant is found from coasts to mountainsides and flowers profusely from midsummer onwards. The striking golden or orange-petalled flowers are followed by slender, somewhat sharply-pointed pods, so it is easy to see how many of the names are derived.

BISTORT, COMMON
(*Persicaria bistorta*)

ENGLISH: Great bistort; Snakeweed; Snakeroot

GAELIC: *Bilur / Biolar / Biolur,* same as *biolar* = watercress

SCOTS: Pencuir kale (Ayrshire); Snake weed (Banff, Lanarkshire)

This edible, peppery plant shares its Gaelic name with the similarly peppery watercress (*Rorippa nasturtium-aquaticum*). The other species of bistorts usually have variants of the name, such as Alpine bistort (*Persicaria vivipara*), which is *Altanach*, or *Biolur ailpeach*. However amphibious bistort (*Persicaria amphibia*) is *glùineach an uisge* or *glùineach dhearg* in Gaelic – the plant with knees that lives in the water, or the red-kneed plant. In Shetland, this same species is 'yallowin' girse' for its use in producing a yellow dye.

BITTERSWEET / WOODY NIGHTSHADE
(*Solanum dulcamara*)

ENGLISH: Mad dog's berries; Poisonberry

GAELIC: *Dreimire gorm* – blue scrambler, from *dreimire* (an obscure reference to climber or scrambler); *Fuath gorm* – blue demon; *Luibh-do-labhairt* – ineffable herb from *luibh* = herb and *do-labhairt* = ineffable, incredible, inexplicable; *Miotag bhuidhe* – yellow nipper/pincher/snapper/biter; *Searbhag mhilis* – bitter sweet from *searbh* = bitter and *milis* = sweet; *Slat ghorm* – blue twig/wand

SCOTS: Pushion berry

This attractive little scrambling plant's names mostly reflect its poisonous berries – hence the reference to demon, pincher or biter. The mention of blue is interesting too as the whole plant has a blueish caste to it – particularly in the velvety hairs on the stems, hence *slat ghorm*. A relative of tomato, it has similar flowers, although the petals are blue. The far smaller berries are reminiscent of tomatoes as they ripen through green, to yellow then red.

BLACKTHORN
(*Prunus spinosa*)

ENGLISH: Sloe

GAELIC: *Airne*; *Airneag*; *Crann-Airneag*; *Craobh-airneag*; *Draighneag*; *Drain*; *Dris*; *Droigheann* – the piercer; *Droigheann-dubh* / *Droighionn dubh* / *Droighneach dubh* – the dark piercer; *Droighneag*; *Preas nan airneag* / *Preas-airneag* – 'Sloe bush' an obsolete name; *Sgitheach dubh* – the fearful black, or a black haw (as in hawthorn) from *sgeach* = a haw; *Sluach*; *Straif* – an obsolete name

SCOTS: Bulister / Bullister; Slae

The classic early flowering hedgerow plant provides two things: sharp bitter sloes for flavouring and piercing wounds from the many large thorns.

BLUEBELL (ENGLISH)
(*Hyacinthoides non-scripta*)

ENGLISH: Hyacinth; Jacintyne; Wild hyacinth; Wood hyacinth

GAELIC: *Bogha muc*; *Fuath-mhuc* – hated/avoided by pigs, as pigs do not eat the bulbs; *Lili ghucagach* – fool's/false lily; *Lus na ginein goraich*; *Lus-na-gineal-goraiche*; *Pubal beannach Brog na cubhaig*

SCOTS: Crantaes; Cra' tae / Craw-taes / Crawtraes – crow's toes; Gowk's hose – cuckoo's/fool's britches or socks

This is the woodland 'English bluebell', but a great many names are shared with the 'Scottish bluebell' (see following entry). Although the two are very different plants from very different habitats, the names have been confused in each language. To add another level of confusion, *Hyacinthoides hispanica* (the Spanish bluebell) is an introduced species that regularly hybridises with *H. non-scripta*.

BLUEBELL (SCOTTISH) / HAREBELL
(*Campanula rotundifolia*)

ENGLISH: Harebell; Lady's thimble / Lady's thimbles; Milkwort – milk plant; Old man's bell – the Devil's bell; Scottish bluebell; Thimbles; Witch bells; Witches' thimbles

GAELIC: *Barr-cluigeannach* – bell-flower; *Brog na cubhaig* – cuckoo's shoes; *Currac cuthaige / Currac na cubhaig / Currachd-na-cubhaige* – cuckoo's cap; *Am Fluran cluigeanach / Pleuran cluigeannach / Pluran-cluigeanach* – bell-like flower; *Fuath-mhuc* – hated/avoided by pigs, although this is more appropriate for the bulb-bearing *Hyacinthoides non-scripta*

SCOTS: Aul' man's bells – the Devil's bells; Blaewort / Blauer / Blaver / Blawort / Blowart. Blue blavers – blue flower; Gowk thimles / Gowk's thimbles / Gowk's thimmles / Gowk's thrimmles / Gowk's thrummles / Gowk's thumles / Gowk's thummles – cuckoo's/fool's thimbles; Gowk's hose – cuckoo's/fool's britches or socks; Lady's thummles / Leddy's thimbles / Leddy's thummles – lady's thimbles; Milkort / Milk-ort – milk-plant

This is the smaller 'Scottish bluebell' from dry, open grasslands rather than the English or Spanish bluebell of woodlands. It is difficult to determine which names certainly belong to which plant. Both have blue, bell-like flowers, both could equally be the cap or socks of a cuckoo or a fool – or a cuckolder. The exception is perhaps *fuath-mhuc* as *C. rotundifolia* would almost never be encountered by forest-dwelling pigs and lacks the unpleasant-tasting bulb of the woodland *H. non-scripta*. Whatever species you consider, bluebells are clearly a salutary lesson in the mutability of names.

BOG ASPHODEL
(*Narthecium ossifragum*)

GAELIC: *Blioch / Bliochan* – milk/milk plant, although obsolete; *Fianach* – moor grass; *Luibh-Chaluim-Chille* – St. Columba's plant; *Lus a chrodain*

SCOTS: Limrek – perhaps limb-wrack/breaker?

This intriguing little moorland plant is one of several plants believed to cause brittle bones in sheep – hence the taxonomic name *Narthecium ossifragum*. The specific epithet means 'bone-breaker', a name possibly reflected in the Scots 'limrek'. It is likely that the acid bogs this plant inhabits are low in available calcium, so sheep grazing there over time would indeed develop brittle bones.

BOG MYRTLE
(*Myrica gale*)

ENGLISH: Gale; Myrtle; Scotch gale; Sweet gale

GAELIC: *Cannach* – fragrant, pretty, mild, soft, beautiful shrub; *Coinneach-dhearg* – red moss, i.e. red *Sphagnum*; *Fionnlach* from *fionn* = white – a name also given to *Sphagnum* moss; *Mointeach liath* – also a name for *Sphagnum* moss; *Rideag* – fragrant with the scent of *M. gale*; *Roid* (Highland); Roideagach (Colonasay)

SCOTS: Gall / Gall-busses (Banffshire); Myrthus

The distinctive bog myrtle is widely lauded for its delightful fragrance – as sweet gale, or *Cannach*. Some accounts suggest the heavenly scent can be used to drive away the dreaded midge, although the jury is out on this one, but it certainly works well as a pot-herb and flavouring in cooking. What is a little strange is the fact that this robust shrub shares names with the tiny bog-mosses (*Sphagnum* species). Aside from living in similar habitats, it is otherwise a very different plant.

BOGBEAN
(*Menyanthes trifoliata*)

ENGLISH: Bog nut; Buckbean (Roxburghshire); Marsh trefoil

GAELIC: *Luibh mhor*; *Luibh-nan-tri-bean* – three-leaved plant (Colonsay); *Luibh-nan-tri-bheann* – plant of the three hills (Colonsay); *Lui'-nan-tri-beann* – trefoil/three-leaved plant; *Lus nan laogh*; *Milsean monaidh* – sweet plant of the hill; *Pacaran chapull* – the mare's packs/wallets; *Pacharan-chapuill* – the mare's pack; *Ponair chapull* – the mare's bean; *Ponair churraig*; *Ponair-churaich* – bog/marsh bean; *Seimh* – pacific and soothing; *Tribhealeach* / *Tri-bhileach* / *Trì-bhileach* – three-leaved plant/trifoliate plant; *Tri-bhilean* – three-leaved plant; *Tri-bileach*

SCOTS: Gulsa-girse – jaundice grass (Shetland); Threefold / Trefold (Shetland); Water triffle

Bogbean is a lovely aquatic plant with fringed petals on its pure white flowers and succulent leaves with three leaflets. An important tonic for general health among other medical uses and (in Shetland) it was used to treat jaundice, so evidently an evocative and important plant. In Gaelic it is sometimes *An tri-bhileach*: THE three-leaved plant, and there are vague suggestions this was St. Patrick's true shamrock – although most plants with three leaflets have been given this honour at one time or another. The lochans and pools in which it grows are common in both the lowlands and hills (to 1,000m in Perthshire), hence the possible references to 'hill plant'.

BORAGE
(*Borago officinalis*)

GAELIC: *Barraisd / Borraidh / Borraisd / Borraist* – from *borr* = become big, bully, swagger, or *borrach* = a great, haughty or proud man and *ago* = to act or effect, or perhaps from *burra* = rough hair, characteristic of this genus. Supposed to give courage and strengthen the action of the heart; *Borage*; *Boraist / Borrach / Borraigh* – a corruption of [*cor* = heat] and *ago* = to act or effect; *Borrach* is also a man of courage

This plant was widely used in European medical traditions and thought of as one of the 'four great cordials'. It was believed to strengthen the heart and inspire courage.

BOX
(*Buxus sempervirens*)

ENGLISH: Boxwood; Bush – perhaps from the French buis/bouis

GAELIC: *Aigh-ban / Craobh-aigh-ban* – *aigh* = happiness, prosperity; *Bocsa / Bosca*; *Crann-bosca* – tree of happiness or prosperity

SCOTS: Buschbome / Buschboun – this may refer specifically to the wood of the plant

As in many Indo-European languages, the Gaelic names are probably a corruption of buxus from the Greek 'buxos'. Variants are widely used throughout Indo-European languages. Although not native to Scotland, box is widely found in gardens and has long been grown and traded for its close-grained wood used in box making (surprise!), cabinetry and marquetry. It has evidently been a part of Scottish society for a long time, as a sprig of box is the botanical clan badge of clan McIntosh, worn as a cockade in the cap or on the breast.

BRACKEN

(*Pteridium aquilinum*)

ENGLISH: Shady bracken

GAELIC: *Bun-dubh* (South Uist, Eriskay); *Bun rainnich*; *Froindeach* (Uist); *Guiseag rainich* – rush-fern/reed-fern; *Raineach* (South Uist, Eriskay); *(An) Raineach mhòr*– (the) big fern; *Raith*; *Roindeach* / *Roineach* (Uist).

SCOTS: Brachan / Brachens; Braikin; Brechan; Brecken; Ern Fern – eagle fern (from pattern of fibres in stalk); Fern; Rannoch – from the Gaelic *Raineach*

One interpretation of the common English name is that 'brack' or 'brake', the general term for ferns in several Germanic languages including English and Scots, has picked up a feminine ending ('in' or 'en'). Bracken was one of the most distinctive ferns and incredibly important as a fertiliser, packing material, bedding for livestock and a host of other things, so it is maybe no surprise that Gaelic and Scots both have broad generic names for it that equate to 'fern', or '*The* fern', or even just 'fern-leaf'. The Gaelic *guiseag raineach* is most likely to be referring to bracken's use as a thatch, similar to rushes or reeds.

In Scots 'Ern fern', relates to either the frond appearing like an eagle spreading its wings, or the pattern of the vascular bundles seen in the stalk of the frond when it is cut, which is said to resemble an eagle's head. This latter explanation may be pushing it a bit, but perhaps if you are cutting thousands of fronds a day for thatching it is easier to spot.

BRAMBLE / BLACKBERRY
(*Rubus fruticosus*)

ENGLISH: Black buttons;
Brambles (Perthshire);
Garter berries

GAELIC: *Brayonan* (Glen Lyon);
Brayoran; *Crion dris*; *Dreas / Dris* –
Cameron suggests it is cognate
with Welsh dy = force/irritation and
rys = to entangle (Cameron, 1883);
Dreach; *Dreas-nan-smeur* – bush
that smears; *Dris-muine / Dris
mhuine* – see description below;
Dris-smeur – bush that smears;
Druise; *An druise beannaichte /
An druise bennaichte*; *Fearra-dhris*;
Grian mhuine – thorn (bush) that
basks in the sun; *Lus-nan-gorm-
dhearc* – entangler; *Muin / Muine* –
vine; *Muir*; *Preas-nan-smeur*;
Smear phreas – bush that smears;
Smearag / Smearagan –smearer/
stainer; *Smeur / Smeuran*; *Smeur
dubh*; *Smeur-a-duihe*; *Smeur-an-
dubha*; *Smeur-dhubh*; *Smeur-
preas*; *Smiaran dubh cf smeur*
(South Uist, Eriskay); *Smior*;
Smior dues (Skye)

SCOTS: Blackboyd / Blackboyds / Black boids / Black boyds (Western Scotland / West Sutherland); Black Bowours (Berwickshire); Blackbides (Kirkcudbrightshire, Wigtownshire); Blackblutters (Hamilton); Blackbyde; Brammie; Brammle; Bumblekites; Drumlie-droits (Perthshire); Garten-Berries (Roxburghshire); Gatter tree (Roxburghshire); Gatter-berries, Gatter-berry (Roxburghshire); Lady garten-berries (Roxburghshire); Lady's gartens / Lady's garters (Roxburghshire); Leddy's gartens / Leddy's garters; Scaldberries

The easy identification and snackability of brambles have given this plant a huge array of names. In Gaelic many of the names refer to the staining juice of the berries or entangling stems. In Scots, the stems as lady's garters perhaps have connotations of entanglements of a different kind. The names recorded in William Patrick's 1831 *A Popular Description of the Indigenous Plants of Lanarkshire*, are a nice trove – 'blackblutters' may refer to the blotting/staining fruit juice, but the prize for the most poetic name surely has to go to 'bumblekites' – likening the fruits to plump bumblebees, with which they share the name.

Bramble or vines represent the letter M as *Muin* in the Gaelic alphabet of tree names.

BROOKLIME
(*Veronica beccabunga*)

ENGLISH/SCOTS: Beccabung; Bekkabung; Horse wellcress; Horse-well-grass; Wall ink; Water purpie; Well ink / Wellink

GAELIC: *Biolair-mhuire* (Colonsay); *Biolar uisge* – watercress; *Lochal* – loch-weed; *Lochal Mothair* – possibly from *modhar* = soft/tender; *Lochal mothair*; *Lothail* – water plant from *lo* = water

This common little plant of still or slow-flowing water was believed to be good for horses – hence horse-well-grass. There are some suggestions that 'purpie' may be a corruption of 'purifier' from the belief that the plant helps clean the water, which to an extent is true. It does also like to grow in relatively clean water, though, but please do not take its presence as meaning water is safe to drink!

BROOM
(*Cytisus scoparius*)

GAELIC: *Bealuidh / Bhealaidh / Bhealuidh* – favoured of Belus / Baal; *Cuilc shleibh* – from *giolc* = reed/cane/leafless twig and *sleibhe* = of the hill, leafless twig of the hill; *Giolach sleibhe* – reed/cane/leafless twig of the hill; *Giolcan*; *Sguab* – a brush made from broom

SCOTS: Breem (NE Scotland); Brome / Broum / Broume; Brume (Angus and Kirkcudbrightshire); Broom-cow, and other variants such as broum-cow, broume-cow

The Gaelic allusions to the gods Belus, or Baal are part of a long and complex chain of connections through many pantheons from the Mediterranean to northern Celtic ones, suggesting the yellow, shining flowers of broom would have been sacred to ancient solar deities. It may indeed be that the Celtic gods Belenos, or Lugh had some strong connection to the plant for this reason, but it may just be Victorian romanticism. It could equally be derived from *bhuidhe* (yellow).

In Scots, he-broom is *Laburnum* – a robust tree that is a fairly close relative of *Cytisus*.

BUGLE
(Ajuga reptans, and possibly *A. pyramidalis)*

GAELIC: *Fiadhain; Glasair choille; Meacan dubh; Meacan dubh fiadhain* – the dusky wild plant

SCOTS: Deid man's bellows (Ayrshire)

This delicate little plant is one of several dead-men's plants – often associated with those plants or fungi that grow low to the ground in shady areas.

BURDOCK
(Arctium minus)

GAELIC: *Bramasag; Cleiteag* – small flakes, quills or feathers; *Dogha* – dock; *Gallan-greannachair* – the rough-haired stalk/plant; *Leadan liosda* – stiff head of hair; *Mac-an-dogha / Meacan-dogha* – mischievous plant; *Meacan-tobhach* – the plant that seizes; *Meacan-tobhach-dubh* – the black plant that seizes; *Searcean* – the beloved person; *Seircean mor* – the great beloved person; *Seircean suirich* – affectionate wooer; *Suirichean suirich* – foolish wooer

SCOTS: Bardog / Burdog (Shetland); Burdocken; Burrs; Flapper bags

This burly member of the daisy family has fruit-heads (the burrs) with the strongest of hooks on them and are famously the inspiration for Velcro. These burrs clothe South Queensferry's Burry man who parades through the town as part of the annual Ferry Fair celebrations in August. The other burdock species native to Britain is greater burdock (*Arctium lappa*) which has only rarely been recorded in Scotland, but the names are largely interchangeable. The similarity to other chunky plants such as dock (*Rumex* species) means some of the names are shared with these as well – the beautifully descriptive 'flapper bags' is a good example, shared with butterbur (*Petasites hybridus*).

BULRUSH
(*Typha latifolia*)

ENGLISH: Cat's tail / Great reedmace / Reed-mace / Reedmace

GAELIC: *Bodan dubh* – little tail or dark tail, dark little tail, or alternatively large tail; *Cuigealach-mhoine* (Beauly and surrounds); *Cuigeal-nam-ban-sith* / *Cuigeal-nam-ban-sithe* / *Cuigeal nam Ban-sìdh* – fairy woman's spindle; *Cuigeal-nan-losgainn* – frog's spindle; *Cuile*

SCOTS: Bull-segg

Seggs are a broad term for 'sedges' – a wide range of grass-like plants, or even the habitats in which they grow, usually wet areas. This is broader than the botanical sedges, members of one particular family, the Cyperaceae. The downy seeds of this plant were used for stuffing pillows.

BUTCHER'S BROOM
(*Ruscus aculeatus*)

ENGLISH: Sutherland broom

GAELIC: *Bealaidh chatach*; *Calg-bhealaidh* – prickly broom; *Calg-bhrudhainn* / *Calg-brudhainn* / *Calg-bhruidhainn, brudhan* / *brughan* may refer to small twigs or may be a corruption of *brum* (broom) and *bruth* or *bruidh* = are sometimes a thorn or prickle; *Calg-cuilc* – point of the prickle

Butcher's broom gets its English name from butchers using it to clean chopping blocks – the stiff stems and pointed, leaf-like cladodes, brushed away gobbets of flesh and flies easily. The plastic greenery you can still see in some butchers' trays, is a throwback to this. It was also the cap-badge of the Sutherland and Chattan clans. It is not native that far north in Scotland, so Clyne (1989) wonders why it was adopted, but has been cultivated and was used medicinally, with the bright red berries seen to symbolise blood, and was widely known.

BUTTERBUR
(*Petasites hybridus*)

ENGLISH: Pestilence-wort; Paddy's rhubarb; Son-before-the-father; Wild rhubarb

GAELIC: *Gallan mòr* – big branch or stalk; *Pobal / Pubal* – tent, cover; *Pubal beannach* – the pinnacled tent

SCOTS: Burn-blade – stream leaf; Dishilago / Tushilago; Eldin-docken; Flapper-bags; Puddock pipe; Sheep-root; Yirnin girse

This large-leaved waterside plant's names overlap with several other species. 'Dishy-lucky', 'son-before-the-father' and 'tushilago' are shared with the much smaller, but similar(-ish) coltsfoot (*Tussilago farfara*). Both these species flower before the heart- or hoof-shaped leaves come out. The similarity of the names butterbur and butterwort (*Pinguicula vulgaris*) has almost certainly led to some confusion over the names 'sheep-root' and 'yirnin girse' being misapplied to butterbur.

BUTTERCUPS
(*Ranunculus* species)

ENGLISH: Fairgrass (Roxburghshire)

GAELIC: *Buidheag* – yellow flower/yellow one; *Buidheag an t-samhraidh* – yellow summer-flower; *Cearban / Fearban / Gaircean / Gairghin* – may all derive from the destroyer; *Cearban feoir* – grass rag for the meadow buttercup (*Ranunculus acris*); *Craglus* (South Uist, Eriskay); *Follasgain*; *Fuile-thalmhainn / Guile thalmhainn* – blood of the earth; *Gair-cean*; *Lus-an-rocais* – crow/rook's plant; *Tuile thalmhainn* – a watercourse or flooded ground; *Torrachas Biadhain* – food to be afraid of

SCOTS: Fox-fit / Fox-fits – fox feet; Goldilocks; Gollan / Golland / Gowan – golden; Craw-feet; Craw taes; Hen-taes; Kraa-tae / Kraatae (Shetland); Sikker; Sit-fast; Sitsicker; Yeller gowan / Yellow gollan

Distinctive, common plants with interesting folklore and an important role as agricultural weeds, it is no surprise the buttercups have adopted a huge array of names. Several of these names are specific to particular species, with the main agricultural weed being creeping buttercup (*Ranunculus repens*). However, any buttercup could legitimately be called gowan or any one of its numerous variants in Scots. This is derived from 'golden', so applies to many other species of yellow-flowered plants. *Buidheag* and *cearban* are both general Gaelic names for buttercups and the derivation is uncertain but do be careful of *cearban* – it is also the name for the basking shark (*Cetorhinus maximus*) – certainly not one to mix up when planning a garden!

Gruag Muire is Mary's locks, specific to the goldilocks buttercup (*Ranunculus auricomis*).

Cameron (1883) suggests that *fuile-* or *guile thalmhainn*, as 'blood of the earth' relates to buttercups 'exhausting the soil'. Crowfoot and allied names across the languages refer to the leaf shape of many species of buttercup, which is reminiscent of a bird's foot.

BUTTERWORT
(*Pinguicula* species)

ENGLISH: Bog violet;
Butter-plant (Selkirkshire)

GAELIC: *Badan-measgain /
Bodan-measgain* – butter mixer;
Brog na cubhaig – cuckoo's shoe;
Lus an bhainne / Lus-a'-bhainne –
milk wort; *Lus an ime* – butter
plant; *Modalan* (Colonsay);
Mòthan; *Mòan* (Skye); *Slim*;
Uachdar – cream

SCOTS: Earning-grass
(Lanarkshire); Ecclegrass –
wet-meadow or island grass
from ic/ig/eig/iccle (Orkney);
Ekel-girse (Orkney, Shetland);
Ostin girse – butter mixer/cheese
plant (Shetland); Rot grass
(Berwickshire); Sheep rot; Sheep-
root (Roxburghshire); Sheep-rot
(N Scotland); Steep-grass – steeped
in milk or water; Yirnin-girse –
curdling plant (Shetland)

Butterwort is a lovely little plant
of bogs, growing in permanently
wet peat. The star-like rosette of
small green leaves traps insects,
breaking down their prey with
digestive enzymes on the surface.
These enzymes made butterwort
ideal for curdling milk, so it was
important for making cheese
and butter, and used on a small
and medium industrial scale.
The sheep-related names pick up
on the habitat where the plants
dwell – if you graze sheep where
this plant grows, they may suffer
from rotting conditions in the feet
and legs.

C

CABBAGE, KALE AND CAULIFLOWER
(*Brassica oleracea*)

GAELIC: *Càl / Càil / Chàil*; *Praiseach* – the pot-herb; cauliflower is *Cal-colag / Cal-colaig / Colag* – little cabbage; *Cal-gruidhean / Cal-gruth*; *Cal-gruthach* – cabbage with curd-, porridge- or grain-like flowers

SCOTS: Bow stock; Bowcail / Bowkail / Bowkaill; Cabbitch-kail (Angus and NE Scotland); Cale / Kail / Kale / Keill / Kell (particularly Angus and NE Scotland); Cauliflooer – cauliflower; Kail blade – the leaf; Kail-runt – the stalk (Shetland and SW Scotland); Loukit kaill – an archaic term; Lucken – a variety with a compact head; Ribe – tall thin cabbage plants; Runk – cabbage stalk (Caithness, Morayshire); Runt; Kilmaurs kail – a hardy late 18th-century variety fed to cattle

Cabbages and kail are hardy, nutritious and easily grown in many settings, including urban kailyards that took their name, so it is easy to see how they came to represent the diet and horticulture of the urban poor throughout the East in particular. More widely in lowland areas, an extensive set of traditions grew up around this important plant, and it was said you could even predict the appearance and traits of your future lover through selecting a cabbage from a pile of them. In Scots, the bow element seen in some names likely comes from baw, or ball – as in a well-developed head. See the entry on Sea kale for related names.

CAMPION, BLADDER OR WHITE
(*Silene latifolia* or *S. vulgaris*)

ENGLISH: Cow-cracker (central and S Scotland)

GAELIC: *Coirean nam balgan* – bag/bladder campion

SCOTS: Coo-cracker; Cowmack / Cow-mack (Dumfriesshire, Ulster)

These attractive members of the carnation family were thought to cause illness in cattle, hence the cow-related names.

CAMPION, RED
(*Silene dioica*)

GAELIC: *Cìrean choilich / Cìrean coilich* – cockscomb; *Coirean coilich / coireann-coillich* – the little cock's cauldron; *Corcach coille* – wood hemp; *Corcan coille* – red woodland flower or little cork of the woodland; *Coirean coilleach*; *Lus-an-rois* – the rose's plant (Colonsay)

SCOTS: Cancer; Sweet Willie (Shetland); William

The Scots names for this widespread and cheerful woodland plant recall its popular garden relative, Sweet William (*Dianthus barbatus*). Most of the Gaelic names are variants on cockerels, referencing the wavy pink-red petals reminiscent of a cock's comb.

CAMPION, SEA
(*Silene maritima*)

GAELIC: *Coirean na mara* – sea campion; *Corragan-an-duine-mhairbh* – dead men's fingers

SCOTS: Buggie-flower (Shetland); Dead man's bells / Deid man's bells; Devil's hatties / Deil's hatties; Sholgirse (Shetland)

The inflated calyx of this delicate coastal plant is reminiscent of a tinkling bell, albeit with a sinister twist in many of these names.

CARAWAY
(*Carum carvi*)

GAELIC: *Carbhaidh / Carbhinn* – from the ancient name; *Lus Mhic Chuimein* – McCumin's wort

SCOTS: Carvie; Carvy

Caraway was widely used throughout western Eurasia as a medicine and spice, so the name carries through a great many languages, and its origins are obscure. *Lus Mhic Chuimein* is an interesting name derived from the similarity between caraway and cumin flavours.

CARRAGEEN
(*Chondrus crispus*)

ENGLISH: Irish moss

GAELIC: *Athair an duileasg / Cairgein, An / Carraceen, An; Mathair an duileasg* – mother of dulse

One of the most important edible seaweeds in Scotland (and not a moss, as one of the common English names suggest), carrageen was used to make the soothing carrageen puddings. Boiled in milk to act as a thickening agent, then flavoured up with vinegar and pepper, lemon juice or similar, it was an ideal food for the recuperating invalid, and still popular today.

CARROT
(*Daucus carota*)

ENGLISH: Bird's nest

SCOTS: Curran petris; Deil in a bush; Mirrot; Muiron-gae; Skirrets

GAELIC: *Carrait* – perhaps a corruption of carrot; *Cearacan*; *Cerrucan* – specifically the root; *Curral*; *Curran* – cur to sow; *Curran* – root like a carrot; *Curran buidhe* – yellow carrot; *Curran Fiadhain*; *Meacan-bhuidhe* – yellow root; *Meacan-raidich*; *Miuran / Muran* – plant with tapering roots, also used for parsnip

The sources of the names for carrot are quite obscure. There is some speculation that the name comes from the Celtic or older Indo-European word 'car' – red, seen in carmine, hence car-root. Several of the Gaelic names are shared with other plants, so *cearacan* is also used for the roots and rhizomes of silverweed (*Argentina anserina*), which were apparently an important source of calories. Similarly, the name *muran* is also used for the unrelated marram grass (*Ammophila arenaria*), renowned for its extensive root-like rhizomes, but may derive from a wider Celtic reference to the seashore, the typical habitat for wild carrots and marram grass. *Meacan* is a large tap root or bulb, and *meacan-raidich* is usually the radish root (*Raphanus* species) but is also recorded in Dwelly (2001) for the carrot.

Deil in a bush, or deil in the bush is a nice reference to the solitary red flower found in the centre of the dense white flowers, all surrounded by a 'nest' of finely divided bracts. It is a name shared with several other species with such fluffy bracts, including the more familiar love-in-a-mist (*Nigella damascena*).

CHAMOMILE
(*Chamaemelum nobile* and other species)

SCOTS: Camomile; Cammavyne / Camouine / Camovine (Angus, NE Scotland)

GAELIC: *A Bhuideag chambil* – yellow chamomile; *Bhuideag shearbh / Buidheag-shearbh* – the bitter yellow flower; *Camabhil / Camomhail / Camomhil* (Colonsay); *Luibh-leighis* – healing plant; *Lus-nan-cam-bhil / Lus-nan-cam-bile*

Chamomile is a name used for several medicinal plants across Europe, so the names reflect their continental names and usually carry through to become local variants of the original French.

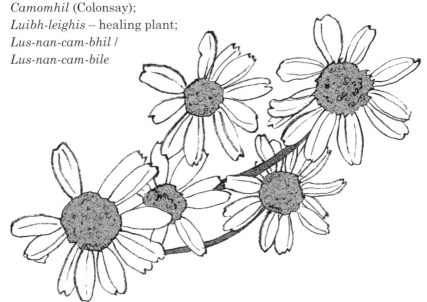

CELANDINE, GREATER
(*Chelidonium majus*)

ENGLISH: Mare's foot; Swallow-wort

GAELIC: *Ansgoch*; *Aonsgoch* – the lonely flower; *Brog na laireach*: *Ceann Ruadh* – reddish head; *Lach ceann-ruadh*

Greater celandine is an archaeophyte – an old non-native introduction to the Scottish flora, found in warmer areas, often associated with limey mortar on old walls. Based on a classical myth that swallows used it to cure blindness in their chicks, the orange-red milky sap was used to treat eye conditions.

CELANDINE, LESSER
(*Ficaria verna*)

ENGLISH: Pilewort; Foalfoot; Herb of St. Ternan

GAELIC: *Grain-aigean*; *Grain-aigein*; *Gràn aigein* – loathsome thing; *Gran arcain* – a cork; *Lion h'aibhne*; *Searragaich* – to bottle; *Searraiche* – (little) bottle roots

SCOTS: Horse-gowan; Solandene

This little woodland herb's leaves are reminiscent of a horse's hooves, but smaller than those of the similar(ish) coltsfoot (*Tussilago farfara*), hence foalfoot. The bottle-shaped roots are very acrid and, looking like nothing so much as a cluster of bottle-shaped haemorrhoids, they were used to treat piles – hence pilewort.

CENTAURY
(*Centaurium erythraea*)

ENGLISH: Gentian

GAELIC: *Ceud bhileach* – hundred-leaved; *Deagha dearg / Deargha dearg* – red wort; *Seamrabhuidha / Seanntraigh / Seantruidh* (South Uist, Eriskay); *Teantguidh / Teantruidh*

SCOTS: Feverfoullie

This delicate little coastal plant is one of relatively few species in the gentian family in Scotland and was used to treat fevers, hence the Scots name. The *ceud bhileach* reference to a hundred-leaved plant may be an erroneous interpretation of an Irish Gaelic name for the plant, or an elaborate mix-up with other plants such as feverfew (*Tanacetum parthenium*) or yarrow (*Achillea millefolium*) used for similar purposes.

In Gaelic, the related seaside centaury is *dreimire mara*, or *dreimire muire*, which is sometimes translated as 'Mary's scrambler'. The lesser centaury is *dreimire bheag*.

CHANNELLED WRACK
(*Pelvetia canaliculata*)

ENGLISH: Calf-weed

GAELIC: *Feamainn chir / Feamainn chireach / Feamainn-chireag / Feamainn-chirean* – comb seaweed

SCOTS: Cow tang

Scots and English names relate to this little strandline seaweed's use in fattening up cattle for market. It lives in the splash zone at the top of rocky shores, so contains a relatively high proportion of fat and protein to survive long periods of drying out. The Gaelic names are more descriptive, all relating to the similarity between the dried seaweed and a comb – albeit a very brittle one!

CHARLOCK
(*Sinapis arvensis*)

ENGLISH: Cherlock; Wild mustard; Yellow-weed

GAELIC: *A mharag* / *Amharag* / *Amharaich a mharaich* / *Am maraiche* – allegedly derived from *amh* = 'raw/uncooked' interpreted as pungent/hot tasting; *An carran-buidhe* – yellow spurrey; *Cas na tunnaig* – the duck's foot; *Cusag*; *Marag bhuidhe* – yellow sausage, the petals are yellow and the fruits are sausage-shaped; *Mharag* – mustard, usually referring to this species; *Praiseach garbh* – rough pot-herb/rough cabbage; *Sceallan* / *Sgealag* / *Sgealag* / *Sgeallan*; *Sgealpach* – biting/slapping/skelping, perhaps of the flavour

SCOTS: Gool; Guil; Guilde; – gold, from the colour of the petals; Reuthie; Runch / Runches / Runchie / Runchik – from old French ronger, to eat; Runch-balls (Roxburghshire, Orkney, Shetland); Sanapé – from Danish senep;

Scaldock / Scaldrick / Scaldricks / Sceldrick / Skaldock / Skeldoch / Skeldock – *possibly* from Irish Gaelic *sgeallagach* (Caithness of the 17th to 19th centuries); Shelloch / Shellochs / Shellock / Shellocks / Skellie / Skellies / Skelloch / Skellocks (NE Scotland); Shirt – apparently from shear, to cut; Wild kail / Wild kale / Wild kales (S Scotland)

This unassuming member of the cabbage family is often seen as a weed, but the sheer wealth of names associated with it attests to that love-hate relationship between farmers and crofters and their weeds. The pungent leaves and fruits make a tasty snack, but numerous ordnances tried to get rid of it as a weed. Fields would be inspected under the auspices of 'Riding the Guilde', to check if any of the golden flowers showed up, and growers would be fined if any of the weeds had escaped their attentions. This is apparently the origin of the Scots 'shirt' – the plant should be sheared, or cut out of the field, although that is a bit of a stretch especially as it was easily pulled out. Gaelic tradition picks up on the weedy nature too – *carran-buidhe* is 'yellow spurrey'; a name to be compared with *carran*, the corn-spurrey (*Spergula arvensis*), another common weed of cornfields with white flowers.

This species is certainly one to read all the names of and delve into their meanings and connections with a huge amount of caution at some of the assumptions that have been made. Clearly there are many orthographic variants, but the way in which people have back-translated many of the names to find a meaning is wonderful. In Gaelic, the variants on *amharag*, and *a mharag* are interpreted as coming from *amh*, meaning 'raw/uncooked', but interpreted very

broadly as 'pungent' by Cameron (1883), Dwelly (2001) and others coming along since. However, one of these variants is *a mharaiche* – 'the sailor'. This is a name also given to scurvy grass, a coastal relative of charlock belonging to the same family, and with the same peppery taste, but otherwise looking completely different with shiny, spoon-shaped leaves and white flowers. Charlock is much taller, with yellow flowers and leaves somewhat reminiscent of a shield, or perhaps a duck's foot if you squint, hence a couple of the other names.

The many variants of skeldock may derive from 'scald-dock' meaning hot dock, as the plant is superficially like docks and sorrels (*Rumex* species) but has a hot rather than 'cooling' taste. Certainly, there is plenty of research that could be done on this one humble plant alone.

CHERRY, BIRD
(*Prunus padus*)

GAELIC: *Craobh fhiodhag* – from *fiodhach* = a shrubby area or wood; *Donn-ruisg / Donn-rusg* – from *donn* = brown and *rusg* = skin or husk; *Fiodhag* – apparently from *fiodh* = wood, although the name is also used for figs; *Fiodhagach / Fiodhagaich*; *Glocan / Glacan* – prong or fork

SCOTS: Hackberry (Berwickshire, Roxburghshire, Dumfriesshire, Perthshire); Hagberry; Hawkberry

This is the smaller-fruited of the two native cherries, and the fruits are a great favourite with birds – the taxonomic name for the other species, *Prunus avium* related to birds. The Scots names are believed to derive from the Saxon 'hag', a hedge, so the 'hawk' in hawkberry is a corruption of this rather than a reference to the raptorial bird – confusing? Such is the way of plant names.

CHERRY, WILD
(*Prunus avium*)

ENGLISH: Gean – from French *guigne*

GAELIC: *Gean*; *Geanais*; *Geanois*; *Silisdear* – this is particularly for the fruit

SCOTS: Gean, Geine, Guind, Merry-tree (Shetland); Sirist

This is the larger-fruited native cherry, and is readily eaten processed into jams and jellies and so the names are remarkably consistent across the languages.

CHESTNUTS
(*Aesculus hippocastanum* and *Castanea sativa*)

ENGLISH: Conker – the seed of horse chestnut (*Aesculus hippocastanum*)

GAELIC: *Castan*; *Chraobh geanm chno*; *Chraobh geanm-chno*; *Craobh-geanmchno* – the tree; *Cno-gheanmnuidh* – the nut; *Geanm-chno* – the nut

Note: These Gaelic names relate to the sweet chestnut (*Castanea sativa*); horse chestnut is simply *Craobh-geanm chno-fiadhaich* – the wild chestnut tree

SCOTS: Chessie; Chestane, Cheston

Neither horse chestnut (*Aesculus hippocastanum*) nor sweet chestnut (*Castanea sativa*) are native to Scotland, so names are inevitably recent and unsurprisingly, revolve around the all-important nut. The horse chestnut is simply the conker tree. The Gaelic names revolving around '*geanm chno*' have a hint of playful translation in them as *geanm* is taken here as meaning chaste, and *cno* or *chno*, a nut. The spines on the outside of the fruit might be seen as some kind of elaborate chastity belt protecting the treasure within, but the pun on the sound of the English 'chestnut' is not lost. Indeed, this may relate to an older derivation of chaste-nut in English, rather than the more commonly cited chest-nut.

CHICKWEED
(*Stellaria media* and others)

ENGLISH: A duck's meat; Chickenweed; Chickenwort; Hen's inheritance

GAELIC: *Fliodh* / *Fliogh* / *Fluth* – wetting, or something excreted (Skye); *Fliodh moire* – Mary's chickweed (South Uist, Eriskay)

SCOTS: Arva / Arvi / Ervi (Shetland); Chickenwir (Shetland); Schickenwir

An important little plant, edible as a fresh snack for humans and livestock, including poultry. The Gaelic names might come from the use of its fresh sap to treat rheumatism, although it often grows in areas where there is a slight seep of water in otherwise dry spots.

CHIVES
(*Allium schoenoprasum*)

GAELIC: *Creamh-gàrraidh* / *Creamh garaidh* – garlic cultivated in a smallholding; *Feuran*; *Saidse*; *Seorsa luis*

SCOTS: Sithe / Sithes / Sives / Syves

A slender-leaved member of the onion family, *Feuran* suggests the similarity between this plant and grass, one word for which is *Feur*.

CLEAVERS
(*Galium aparine*)

ENGLISH: Catch-rogue; Goosegrass, Grip-grass; Lizzie in the hedge; Robin-run-in-the-hedge; Sticky grass, Sticky Willie

GAELIC: *Garbh-lus* / *Lus-garbh* – rough weed; *Luibh an ladhair* – claw or catch weed; *Luibh na cabhraich* / *Luibh na cabhruich* *Luibh-na-cabhrach* – possibly nuisance weed (Colonsay)

SCOTS: Bleedy tongue / Bloodtongue/ Bloodytongue; Catchweed; Grip-grass; Gruppit grass; Guse grass; Loosy-tramps; Robbie-rin-the-hedge / Robin-rin-the-hedge; Stickers (Fife, Wigtownshire, Roxburghshire); Sticky grass; Sticky Willie / Sticky Willy; Tongue-bluiders (Berwickshire); Willie rin hedge / Willie rin the hedge (Banffshire, Lanarkshire); Witherspail (Roxburghshire)

A classic plant that's a favourite with children, and one that everyone remembers into adulthood. The hooked surfaces allow it to catch onto clothing and hair, or even draw blood if rubbed on the tongue, hence the name bleedy tongues. This doubtless comes about as a result of playground games, which can be notoriously cruel at times.

CLOUDBERRY
(*Rubus chamaemorus*)

ENGLISH: Dwarf mountain bramble – applied to several alpine brambles

GAELIC: *Cruban na saona*; *Eighreag / Eighreag gae / Faigreag / Feireag / Foighreag / Lus nan eidhreag / Lus nan eighreag / Lus nan Oighreag / Oidhreag / Oighreag / Oireag*; *Muin na mnà-mine* – the gentlewoman's vine (obsolete); *Preas-fhiontag* – hairy shrublet or bush

SCOTS: Averin, Evron (NE Scotland); Aivrons – wild berry; Everocks / Evron (Banff, Moray); Fintock (Perthshire); Knot / Knotberry / Knoutberry; Noop / Noops / Nub / Nub berry (Borders, Berwickshire, Dumfriesshire)

Many of the Gaelic names for this lovely little upland plant derive from *eireachd*, 'beauty' or 'elegance', according to Clyne (1989), although the word can also refer to a meeting or cluster, which nicely describes the clustered orange drupelets of the raspberry-like fruit. MacBain (1982), however, suggests these names derive from the Scots 'averin', this does need more of a leap of the imagination though.

CLOVERS
(*Trifolium* species)

ENGLISH: Wild clover

GAELIC: *Bhealaidh*; *Deocan /
Deochdan* – to suck; *Luibh nan
tri bheann* – three-leaved plant;
Meillonem – honey-wort; *Saimir /
Sameir / Seamair*; *Seamar chapuill* –
mare's clover, possibly of red
clover; *Seamrag / Siomrag*;
Sùgag – a little sup i.e. of the
nectar; *Tri-bhileag / Tri-bilean* –
trefoil/three-leaved plant

SCOTS: Claver (Ayrshire);
Clever – an archaic term; Cow-
cloos; Cow-grass (Roxburghshire);
Curl-doddy (Orkney); Plyvens;
Souk / Soukie / Soukie soo / Soukies /
Suckie / Sucklers (Selkirkshire) /
Sukie; Triffle – from trefoil

Many of the Gaelic names are
shared with other trefoil-bearing
plants such as wood sorrel
(*Oxalis acetosella*) but *bhealaidh* is
normally broom (*Cytisus scoparius*)
and refers to a range of other yellow
things as well, where relatively few
clovers have yellow flowers. That
said, broom and clover are both
members of the pea family, so there
may be a further connection there.
In both Gaelic and Scots, there are
allusions to the sugar hit that could
be gained by supping or sooking on
a freshly plucked clover-head.

An intriguing one is the mention
of 'curl-doddy', a name that is
more commonly applied to ribwort
plantain (*Plantago lanceolata*)
and references the Charleses and
Georges from the Jacobean and
Hanoverian dynasties respectively.
However, 'doddie' in this case
may refer to a head, as several
other plants with this name
have similarly fluffy or curly
flowerheads.

The two most common clovers in
agriculture are white (*Trifolium
repens*) and red (*T. pratense*). Gaelic
names to distinguish them use the
same colours, so *seamrag bhàn*
for white, and *seamrag dearg* for
red. Red clover was also known
as *deochan dearg* or *seirg*. White
clover had several other names,
listed in the specific entry below.

CLOVER, BIRDSFOOT
(*Trifolium ornithopodioides*)

ENGLISH: Birdsfoot fenugreek /
Fenugreek, Greek-nettle

GAELIC: *Crubh-eòin*; *Deanntag
Ghreugach* / *Lonntag greugach* –
Greek nettle; *Fineal greugach* –
Greek fennel (i.e. Fenugreek)

SCOTS: Cammock – perhaps from
Gaelic *cam* = crooked; Catcluke –
cat's claws; Craw-taes – crow's toes

This plant is very rare in Scotland –
appearing as an occasional weed,
but it shares many names with
the similar fenugreek (*Trigonella
feonum-graecum*), and the far more
common bird's foot trefoil (*Lotus
corniculatus*).

CLOVER, HARE'S-FOOT
(*Trifolium arvense*)

GAELIC: *Cas maidhiche* /
Cas maighiche – hare's foot

CLOVER, WHITE
(*Trifolium repens*)

ENGLISH: Dutch clover

GAELIC: *Bileag chapaill*;
Seamair-bhàn – white shamrock;
Seamrag bhàn; *Seamrag geal* /
Seamrag gheal (Colonsay);
Seamrag-an-deocadain / *Seamrag-
an-deocain* – refers to shamrock
and a substance vomited by foals;
Seamrag-nam-buadh – shamrock
of virtues; *Seamrag-nan-each* –
horses' shamrock; *Seamrag-nan-
searrach* – colts' shamrock

SCOTS: Milkies (Morayshire);
Sheepie-mae (N Scotland); Sheep's
gowan; Smara / Smoora (Shetland);
White sookies (Angus and
southwards)

White clover shares many of the
names for other clover species,
found in the general entry
above, but these listed here are
specifically recorded for this, the
most common and agriculturally
important species.

CLUB RUSH, COMMON
(*Schoenoplectus lacustris*)

ENGLISH: Lake club-rush

GAELIC: *Bog* – perhaps from marsh, fen, swampy ground; *Bog luachair* – bog rush; *Bog mhuine / Bog muine* – soft one of the marsh; *Boigean* – marsh, fen, swampy ground; *Buigneach* – bulrush or any aquatic plant; *Cuilc*; *Curcais* – from *curach* = marsh/hair/bulrush; *Gobhal luachair* – forked rush, from *gobhal* = a fork); *Luachair bhogain* (Colonsay); *Luachair ghòbhlach* – forked rush; *Luachair-bhog* – soft rush; *Min-fheur* – soft grass; *Sibhin*

A widespread and common member of the sedge family, it is recognisable by its forked flowerheads. Cameron (1883) suggests that the Gaelic *bog* may derive from the word meaning to wag, which this plant does, rather than bog meaning a marsh.

CLUBMOSSES
(*Lycopodium* species and *Huperzia selago*)

GAELIC: *Garbhag an sleibhe / Garbhag an t-slèibhe* – rough one of the hill is *Huperzia selago*; *Crotal-nam-madadh-ruadh / Crotal-nam-madaidh-ruadh* – dye-lichen of the fox; *Garbhrag-nan-gleann* – rough plant of the glens is *Lycopodium* species; *Lus a' bhalgair / Lus bhalgaire* – fox's plant

SCOTS: Fox-fit / Fox-fits; Tod-tail

Several species of clubmoss are lumped under the same names, distinguished based on their habitat. The smaller, more upright fir-clubmoss (*Huperzia selago*) is *Garbhag an t-slèibhe* (of the hills) distinct from the *Lycopodium* species found at lower altitudes, known as *Garbhag-nan-gleann*. *Lycopodium* means 'wolf's foot'. Given wolves were almost certainly hunted to extinction in Scotland by the time many names were being recorded, the connection with foxes makes more sense in recent centuries.

COLTSFOOT
(*Tussilago farfara*)

ENGLISH: Son before father

GAELIC: *Athan* – firelighter; *Bileag-an-spuine* – little tinder leaf; *Billeog an spuinc*; *Cluas liath* – grey leaf; *Crannaghalan* (South Uist, Eriskay); *Duilliur* – leaf; *Duilliur spuine / Duilliur-spuing* – tinder leaf; *Fathan* – fire/firelighter; *Galan* (South Uist, Eriskay); *Gallan-greannach / Gallan greannchair* – fluffy stem; *Gormag liath* – little light blue one/greyish-green; *Spuinc / Spuing*

SCOTS: Cow-heave / Cow-heaves (Selkirkshire); Dishilago; Dog's chamomile; Doo-docken (Caithness); Dove-lock; Foal foot / Foal's foot (Caithness); Son-afore-the-father (Berwickshire, Roxburghshire); Son-afore-the-faither; Shilagie (Angus, Lanarkshire); Tushylucky; Tushy-lucky gowan (Dumfriesshire)

Many of the names for this little member of the daisy family relate to its wider names across Europe, derived from 'tussilago', meaning inducing coughs. The plant was, and still is, used to treat chest complaints, most famously as a tobacco substitute, and it was a useful firelighter when dried, with the downy white hairs on the leaves and fruits catching light easily, although it was sometimes steeped in other accelerants. 'Son before the father' is because the flowerheads appear before the leaves.

COMFREY
(*Symphytum*)

ENGLISH: Knitbone

GAELIC: *Meacan dubh* – large, dark plant

SCOTS: Banwort

Irish Gaelic names are *Meacan-dubh-calgach* – black plant for broken bones or *Lus nan cnamh briste* – plant for broken bones. The plant was indeed widely used for helping set broken bones.

CORIANDER
(*Coriandrum sativum*)

GAELIC: *Coireaman*; *Lus a choire*

SCOTS: Corrydander (Aberdeenshire, Lanarkshire)

A non-native spice, but one that grows happily in Scotland. The Gaelic names are probably derived from corruptions of the widespread European names for this plant, many of which are similar, so direct translations do not necessarily make sense.

CORNFLOWER
(Centaurea cyanus)

ENGLISH: Bluebottle;
Blue bonnets

GAELIC: *Currac-cubhaige*;
Gille-gorm / Gille-guirmean –
the blue lad; *Gorman*

SCOTS: Blawort; Blaewort;
Blue gomments; Blaver;
Lady's thummles

This cheerful little weed of
cornflowers is a relatively rare
sight nowadays due to the intensive
farming practice of recent times,
although this seems to be reversing
as field margins are given more
space, and in some areas whole
fields are cultivated as a cover crop.

COTTONGRASS
(*Eriophorum* species)

ENGLISH: Cotton sedge;
Hare's tail

GAELIC: *Caineachan*; *Canac-an t-sleibhe* – mountain soft head;
Canach – soft head or perhaps from *can* = white; *Caoin cheann* – from *caoin* = soft and *ceann* = head;
Ceann-ban-a'-mhonaidh – white head of the mountain; *Sgathag fhiadhain / Sgathog fiadhain* – wild little tail; *Sìoda monaidh* – mountain silk from *sioda* = silk and *monadh* = mountain range

SCOTS: Cannach down; Cat tail / Cat's tail / Cat's tails (Aberdeenshire); Draw moss; Drawling; Lukki's oo (Shetland); Mois; Mont grass; Month grass; Moss; Moss-crops; Mossing (Renfrewshire, Lanarkshire); Mount grass / Mounth grass; Pull ling (S Scotland); Purlaing (Berwickshire / Peebles area); Wild cotton

The distinctive cottony white tops of these sedges were used for stuffing mattresses and for staunching wounds. They were collected in great quantities during the First and Second World Wars to make dressings in a similar way to *Sphagnum* moss, which is found in similar wet, peaty habitats.

COUCH GRASS
(Elytrigia repens)

ENGLISH: Twitch; Scutch

GAELIC: *Bruim-fheur* – flatulent or fart-grass; *Feur a' phuint* – grass with points or joints; *Feur-nan-con* – dog's grass; *Fioran / Fiorthan* – detestable; *Goin / Goinean* – a wound, hurt, twitch; *Goin-fheur* – dog's grass; *Punnt* – from Latin *punctum* = a point

SCOTS: Dog-grass; Pirl grass – from pyrl a needle; Ket; Lonnach / Lonnachs (Kirkcudbrightshire, Angus); Quicken-grass / Quickens (central, E and SW Scotland); Rammock; Reemick; Ronnach / Ronnachs (Kirkcudbrightshire); String girse

This wonderfully weedy grass was (and still is) the bane of farmers and gardeners, as some of the names suggest. The running rhizomes produce new plants at most of the jointed nodes, so it is very difficult to eradicate. Hence string girse and quicken grass – with 'quick' being lively and vigorous. Lonnach was the name given to bundles of it gathered for burning.

CRANESBILLS
(*Geranium* species)

GAELIC: *Creachlach dearg* –
the red wound-healer; *Crobh-
priachain* – the raven's claw;
Curran nan caothrach – the sheep's
carrot; *Lus-gnath-ghorm* –
common blue plant

These names all traditionally refer
to bloody cranesbill a showy
species with pink flowers common
on beaches and machair. However,
several of the smaller or more
obscure cranesbills have just a single
'semi-official' Gaelic or English name
as they are seldom distinguished as
noteworthy except to botanists:

Crobh preachain mìn is the dove's
foot cranesbill (*Geranium molle*)

Crobh preachain geàrrte is the
cut-leaved cranesbill (*Geranium
dissectum*)

Crobh preachain deàlrach is the
shining cranesbill (*Geranium
lucidum*)

Two odd exceptions to this are
crobh preachain an lòin, the
meadow cranesbill, which is
striking and common, but often
conflated with the very similar
Geranium sylvaticum, which is,
of course, *crobh preachain coille*.

CROWBERRY
(*Empetrum nigrum*)

GAELIC: *Breallandubh* –
black vessel; *Caor fionnaig* /
Caor-feannaig / *Caora-feannaig* –
crow berry; *Caora fithich* –
raven's berry; *Caora-bhuthagan*
(South Uist, Eriskay) – crowberry;
Caora-fiadhag – black heath berry;
Dearc fhithich / *Dearcfhithich* –
raven's berry; *Dearcan feanaig*;
Dearc-an-fiona / *Dearc-fhiona* –
wine berry; *Fineag* / *Fionag*;
Fionnagan – from *fionnag* = a crow;
Lus na fiadha / *Lus na fiannag* /
Lus na fionnag / *Lus-na-feannaig* /
Lus-na-fionnaig – crow's plant;
Lus na stalog / *Lus-na-staolaig* –
starling's plant; *Preas-nam-fiontag* –
crow's bush

SCOTS: Berry hedder
(Shetland); Berry-girse; Berry-
grass; Blackberry (Caithness);
Crake berries; Crawberry; Craw-
croobs; Craw-croops; Crawcroups;
Croupert; Crowpert; Heather
berry (Dumfriesshire, Ulster
Scots); Heather-berr (Caithness,
Aberdeen); Hillberry (Caithness);
Knauperts (Banffshire); Knowperts
(NE Scotland)

This heathland plant's dark berries
are a bit sour and unpalatable,
but were eaten, sometimes made
into jams, as well as being used as
a dye.

CUCKOO FLOWER / LADY'S SMOCK
(*Cardamine pratensis*)

GAELIC: *Biolair* – a name for any cress, *cardamine*; *Biolair-ghriagain* – bright sunny dainty/daisy; *Brog-na-cubhaige* – the cuckoo's shoe; *Cularan* – perhaps from *culair* = palate or *culear* = a bag; *Flur na cubhaig / Frog na cubhaig* – cuckoo's hole; *Pluir na cubhaig* cuckoo flower; *Gleoran / Gleorann* – pretty, neat, trim or handsome (from *gleoite*); *Lus-an-fhogair*

SCOTS: Carsons; Meadow; Kerses; Spink

The dainty little cuckoo flower dwells in wet meadows and shows its pale lilac petals in late April and May at the time the cuckoo returns from its winter migration, hence the name. The Gaelic *Lus-an-fhògair* (here *fhogair*) is also used for water-pepper (*Persicara hydropiper*) – another peppery-leaved plant of wet meadows.

CURRANT, BLACK
(*Ribes nigrum*)

ENGLISH: Blackberry (Berwickshire); Wineberry

GAELIC: *Dearc dhubh / Dearcan dubh / Dearc-an-dubha* – *dearc* = a berry and *dubh* = black; *Preas-nan-dearc* – the berries' bush; *Raosar dubh* – black raisin from French and English 'raisin'; *Spriunan*

SCOTS: Black raser / Black rissert / Black rizar / Black rizzar; Black russle; Rizzar – 'raisin' from the fruit

The classic bushfruit – with almost every name relating to the precious berries which are used for all manner of desserts and historically, a medicinal wine.

D

DABBERLOCKS
(*Alaria esculenta*)

ENGLISH: Edible kelp

GAELIC: *Birse* – bruise or push;
Cas dhubh – the stem-like stipe;
Duilleach – the membranous frond;
Earball-saile – the reproductive
receptacles; *Gruaigean* (Skye);
Miorcan (Lewis); *Mircean* – possibly
from Norse meaning Mary's kernel,
also used for some red seaweeds;
Muirirean / Muiririn; *Rusg* –
the reproductive receptacles

SCOTS: Badderlocks;
Bladderlocks; Dabberlacks (NE
Scotland); Hen-ware; Hinniwirs
(Shetland); Hinnywaar (Shetland);
Hinnywar / Honeyware / Honey-
ware (Orkney); Keys (Orkney);
Mirkles / Murlins – the inner stem
or laminar midrib of the frond
(Orkney)

Most seaweeds are simple fronds
or filaments, but the robust-yet
elegant brown alga known as
'dabberlocks' is an exception.
It is more elaborate than most
seaweeds, with several weird and
wonderful structures, each of
which was given a name. To the
connoisseur, each of these parts
has a distinct flavour and culinary
use as well. An interesting one is
'keys', probably referring to the
receptacles as they do look like
nothing so much as a bunch of
keys. These are salty, crunchy
and excellent for flavouring stews.

Several of the names look to have
been shared among the languages,
with a hint of a Norse origin for
many, as Orkney and Shetland
have such a wealth of names.
Indeed, the English common name
is likely borrowed from these roots.

Although listed under English –
bladderlocks is likely a variant
of badderlocks and dabberlocks.
This species has no air bladders to
help it to float, but there is a hint
here of the word converging with
'bladderwrack' – another robust
brown seaweed. Waar, or ware is a
general term for similar seaweeds,
and the names inevitably flow into
each other.

DAFFODIL
(*Narcissus* species)

ENGLISH: Lent lily; Lily; White lily; Yellow lily

GAELIC: *Lus a chromchinn* / *Lus-a-chrom-chinn* – plant of the drooping head; *Lus-a'-chinn* – plant of the head; *Lus-an-aisige*

SCOTS: Glen; Glenayrs; Lillie

The striking flowers of daffodils, widespread in gardens or as escapees, seem to have taken the place of lilies in much of Scotland's conscience. They are of course 'St. David's Lily', so more closely associated with Wales, but their significance as a religious stand-in for lilies comes through in several of the names.

DAISY
(*Bellis perennis*)

ENGLISH: Day's-eye, Marguerite

GAELIC: *Buidheag* – the little yellow one (Perthshire); *Dithean*; *Eointean* (Uist); *Gugan* – of the bud or flower; *Neoineag* / *Neòinean* / *Noinean* – the noon-flower from *noin* = noon; *Onaig*; *Paidirean* – a string of beads, the daisy chain (Argyll)

SCOTS: Bairnwort; Benner gowan (Dumfriesshire); Cockiloorie; Curl-doddy – curly head (SW Scotland); Daseyne – a variant used in a 16th-century rhyme; Ewe-gollan / Ewe-gowan; Golland (Caithness); Gowan (Berwickshire); Kokkeloorie / Koukeleri (Shetland); Mary Gowlan (Berwickshire); May Gowan (Angus, Berwickshire); Wallie

Daisies are instantly recognisable, and widely used for making chains; it is one of many 'gowans' in Scots. There is a bit of debate over the source of the name, where gowan possibly comes from the old Scots for a halo, or may be derived from 'golden' the two are likely linked. The Gaelic *dithean* is used in a similar way to gowan, or the English word 'daisy' applied to a wide range of daisy-like plants. A gowany or gowanie lawn is one covered in daisies.

DANDELION
(*Taraxacum officinalis* and other species)

ENGLISH: Dandylion, Daintylion; Devil's milk-plant (Kirkcudbrightshire); Pee-the-bed; What o'clock is it?

GAELIC: *Bearnan bearnach* – fissured notch (very notched); *Beàrnan brìde* – notch-in-leaf/sap or St. Bride's notched one; *Beàrnan brìd* – bright sap; *Bearnan Brighde* – Bridget's notched plant; *Bior nam bride* – sharp/tooth-like sappy plant; *Blath-buidhe* – yellow blossom; *Caisearbhan* – bitter; *Caisearbhan-nam-muc* / *Caistearbhan nam muc* – the pig's bitter plant; *Feacal leaohain*/ *Fiacaill-leòmhainn* / *Fiacal leomhain* – lion's teeth

SCOTS: Bitter aks; Bum-pipe / Bumming pipe (Banffshire, Lanarkshire); Dainties (Banffshire); Deil's milk-pail; Dentylion; Doon-head clock; Eksis girse (Shetland); Horse gowan; Medick (Banffshire); Methick; Milk-gowan; Piss-a-bed / Pisstebed / Pish the bed; Stink Davie (Clackmannanshire); White gowan; Witch gowan; Yellow gowan

Well. Where to start with this cornucopia of names? This is the rarest of plants – which might seem a strange statement, but it is not because it is difficult to find, quite the opposite in fact. This incredibly common and fun little weed can be identified by almost anyone from the age of two, and *that* is a rare thing in modern botany. Combined with its use in traditional medicine this means the dandelion has a plethora of names given to it by everyone from kids to apothecaries. Many of them can be intuited back to their source, and it is a textbook example of how names change. French features as a source of the leonine name 'dandelion', derived from the long, pointed tooth-like taproot – the 'dent de lion', but this becomes 'dainty lion', which could readily describe the mane of yellow florets. Dent-de-lyon is an archaic name when French was a courtly language in 16th-century Scotland, but here the lyon may be an archaic spelling of the beast, or refer to the French city.

A direct translation of the lion's tooth appears in Gaelic, but a whole plethora of names that are mistranslations or orthographic variants appear around the idea of a plant of St. Bride (Brigid), variants of which allude to the notches on the leaves, the sappiness of the plant or simply the saint herself.

Like other golden-flowered members of the daisy family, this is one of the 'Gowans', but for some reason the name 'white gowan' is

recorded for this species. This is either an error as the petals are universally yellow, or it may refer to the white parachute-like fruits, used to tell the time. Each blow on the fruiting head equates to one hour, hence the names 'doon head clock' and 'what o'clock is it?'

Several names reference the bitter, milky white sap, which was and is a diuretic, hence the bedwetting references. It is interesting to see the slight undercurrent of danger in the mentions of the Devil, and many people even now know the childhood story that if you so much as touch the plant it'll be a change of sheets that night (even if they do not believe it). Contrast this with the Gaelic references to St. Bride.

Bum, and bumming pipe refer to the humming noise that can be made with the hollow flower stalk, or peduncle, but always gets a scurrilous laugh, in spite of its innocent origins.

OK – time to stop as we've gone on too long, but as you can see, there is an extensive set of research, with many possible rabbit holes to go down before we untangle this fascinating skein of names.

DARNEL
(*Lolium temulentum*)

ENGLISH: Cockle

GAELIC: *Breòillean* – knotty, perhaps from the knotty appearance of spikes; *Cuiseach* – reed/rush/bulrush; *Paidirean-arbhair* – corn garland from *paidirean* = garland and *arbhar* = corn; *Siobhach-puinnseanta* – poison ryegrass; *Stùrdan* – vertigo/a disease of sheep

SCOTS: Dornell; Roseager / Roseegar

Darnel is relatively rare in Scotland but was previously more common as a weed among the very similar-looking wheat (*Triticum*). Darnel is poisonous, causing disorientation and death in extreme cases, so was notorious throughout Europe and often interpreted as a tool of the Devil, who was believed to sow it among wheatfields. This is possibly the origin of the Gaelic *Stùrdan* – from the similarity in symptoms between the poisoning and staggering in sheep. Most of the other Gaelic names are more generic for grasses and grass-like plants. 'Cockle' is probably a term for a poisonous plant, as is seen in another toxic weed, the corncockle (*Agrostemma githago*).

DEADNETTLE, RED
(*Lamium purpureum*)

ENGLISH: Red archangel

GAELIC: *Caoch-dheanntag dhearg* – red dead nettle; *Deanntag dhearg*/*Ionntag dhearg* – red nettle; *Neanntag aog* (Colonsay)

SCOTS: Daa-nettle / Dee-nettle; Okkerdu (Shetland)

This member of the mint family is somewhat nettle-like, but with pink two-lipped flowers and lacking stings.

DEADNETTLE, WHITE
(*Lamium album*)

ENGLISH: Dead nettle; Day nettles

GAELIC: *Deanntag bhan*; *Deanntag mharb*; *Ionntag bhan* – white nettle; *Ionntag marbh* – dead nettle; *Teanga mhin* – smooth tongue

SCOTS: Deidnettle

The white deadnettle looks very like a true nettle but with large white flowers and no stings, as it is almost completely unrelated. As with the red deadnettle, the names are all derived from translations of the English.

DEERGRASS
(*Trichophorum cespitosum*)

ENGLISH: Deer hair / Deer's hair; Heath club-rush

GAELIC: *Broch-fheur* (Colonsay); *Cìob* / *Cìpe* – food; *Cìob cheann dubh* – black-headed food; *Cruach luachair* – hill-rush; *Ultanaich*

SCOTS: Ling

This tufted sedge is very common on upland areas, so is a key part of the late winter and spring diet of sheep. It is likely that several other plants are lumped in with this under these names. The Scots name 'ling' is a strange one as it is usually applied to one of the heathers (*Calluna vulgaris*), a plant often found with deergrass.

DOCK
(*Rumex* species – the large ones)

ENGLISH: Docken

GAELIC: *Copach* – bossy (Cameron, 1883) or 'little foamy one' (Clyne, 1989); *Copag*; *Copag chamagach* – curled dock, from *camagach* = like ringlets; *Copag leathann* – the broad dock; *Cuiseag ruadh* (South Uist, Eriskay)

SCOTS: Bulmint (Shetland); Bulwand (Shetland); Cushycows (Berwickshire); Dockan / Docken / Dockene; Rantytanty (Ayrshire); Red shank / Redshank / Reidshank / Ridshank; Smari dock

Docks are widely known as an apparent antidote to nettle stings, so it is perhaps a bit surprising not to see any names relating to those, but to their reputation as deep-rooted agricultural weeds, and similarity to other plants such as redshank (*Persicaria maculosa*). The most common species is *Rumex obtusifolius* (the broad-leaved dock) but on the coast, the more slender, wavy-leaved *Rumex crispus* (the curled dock) is commonly found. Some of these names overlap with those for sorrel (*Rumex acetosa*), a smaller relative of these chunky species. Further names for sorrel can be found in its separate entry.

DOG'S MERCURY
(*Mercurialis perennis*)

GAELIC: *Lus an glinne* / *Lus ghlinne* – perhaps cleansing plant, or pretty plant; *Lus ghlinne Bhracadail*; *Lus-glen-Bracadale* (Skye)

SCOTS: Mercury leaf

This member of the spurge family is widespread in old woodland habitats in the lowlands, but less common in the north and west. Used as a 'mercury' to clean suppurating wounds and to induce salivation, this was an important but dangerous medicinal plant. On Skye, it is known from several spots, including Glen Bracadale in the west, which makes for an interesting conflation of *ghlinne* (cleanser) and *glen* referring to the glen from which it was harvested.

DUCKWEEDS
(*Lemna* species)

GAELIC: *Gran lachan* – duck's grain or seeds; *Lus-gun-mhathair-gun-athair* – motherless, fatherless plant; *Mac gun athair* – son without father; *Ros lachain* / *Ros lachan* – duck's rose

Duckweeds are tiny aquatic plants that sit unrooted on the surface of still waters, multiplying seemingly magically – hence some of the Gaelic names. Cameron (1883) has a more elaborate interpretation involving a corruption of *meacan* interpreted as 'still air', but Clyne (1989) and others suggest this is 'perverse' and stretching a linguistic point too far. There are several species of *Lemna* in Scotland, with the names above interchangeable for most. The fat duckweed (*Lemna gibba*) is also known as gibbous duckweed, or *aran tunnaig* in Gaelic.

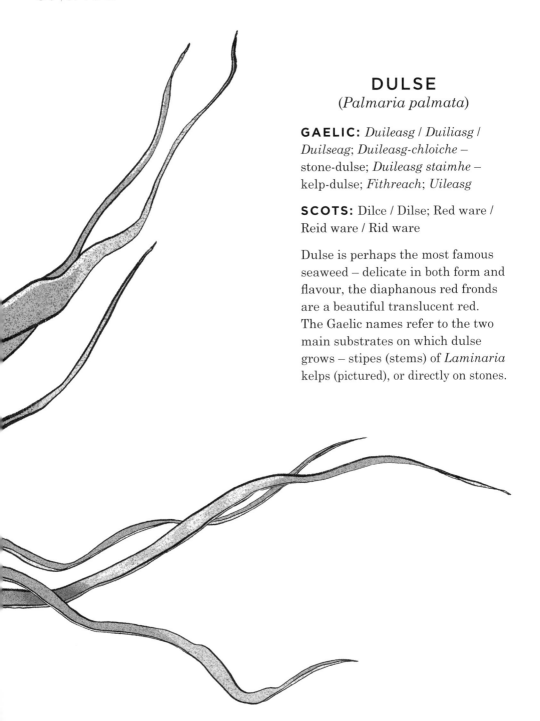

DULSE
(*Palmaria palmata*)

GAELIC: *Duileasg / Duiliasg / Duilseag*; *Duileasg-chloiche* – stone-dulse; *Duileasg staimhe* – kelp-dulse; *Fithreach*; *Uileasg*

SCOTS: Dilce / Dilse; Red ware / Reid ware / Rid ware

Dulse is perhaps the most famous seaweed – delicate in both form and flavour, the diaphanous red fronds are a beautiful translucent red. The Gaelic names refer to the two main substrates on which dulse grows – stipes (stems) of *Laminaria* kelps (pictured), or directly on stones.

E

EELGRASS
(*Zostera* species)

ENGLISH: Sweet sea-grass, Grasswrack

GAELIC: *Bileanach / Bilearach* (Argyll) – from *bileag* = a blade of grass; *Bilearach na Duilleige Caoile* – narrow leaved eelgrass (*Zostera angustifolia*); *Mileanach*

SCOTS: Mallow (Orkney); Marlak / Marlie (Shetland)

Some of the few flowering plants found in marine environments, eelgrass was formerly an important thatching material and was said to last longer than straw. No longer used as such, the estuarine habitats in which it grows are now threatened by fertiliser runoff from the land and shifting sea temperatures.

ELDER
(*Sambucus nigra*)

GAELIC: *Buthraidh* (Wester Ross); *Caor-dhromain / Crann-dromain*; *Droman / Druman / Troman*; *Dromanach / Drumanach*; *Rath fas* – from *rath* = prosperity or good luck and *fas* = to increase; **Ruis** – of the tree or the wood; *Truim crann*

SCOTS: Boon-tree; Bore tree / Boretree / Bore-tree; Borral; Bountree / Boun-tree; Bourtree; Bour-tree; Eller (S Scotland)

Across much of northern Europe, Elder was a magical tree – in some cultures cursed, and others blessed. In Scotland, it is a bit of both, but usually looked on in a favourable light as it was thought to keep away witches, and cutting it down was considered bad luck. This may be reflected in names such as *rath fas* and perhaps 'boon-tree'. On the other hand, the 'boor' and 'bore' elements of the Scots names likely refers to

the soft pith inside the wood of the tree, as this can easily be pushed or bored out, leaving a versatile pipe or tube, so 'boon' may be a further development of these names. In any case, such names have certainly been around since the 16th century. **The name *ruis* represents the letter R in the Gaelic alphabet of tree names.**

ELM
(*Ulmus* species)

GAELIC: *Ailm*; *Crann-leamhain* / *Craobh-leamhain* – elm tree; *Leamhan*; *Liobhan*; *Slamhan*

SCOTS: Elme

Elm in Scotland is mostly represented by the native *Ulmus glabra* – wych elm, and was traditionally used for making water pipes and sewers. **The elm represents *Ailm*, the letter A in the Gaelic alphabet of trees.**

EYEBRIGHTS
(*Euphrasia* species)

GAELIC: *Briollan*; *Caoimin* – from an obsolete word for cleaning; *Glan-ruis* – eye cleanser; *Linn-radharc*; *Lus nan leac* – hillside plant; *Rainn an uisge* / *Rein an ruisg*; *Reing-an-ruisg* – water for the eye; *Ragharcin*; *Soillse-nan-sul* / *Soillseachd-nan-sul* – that which brightens the eye

Dainty little eyebright flowers look exactly as the name suggests, like a bright little eye, so the plant was used to treat eye complaints under the widespread Doctrine of Signatures medicinal system; the theory that if a plant resembles a body part or a condition, it could be used to treat it.

F
to
J

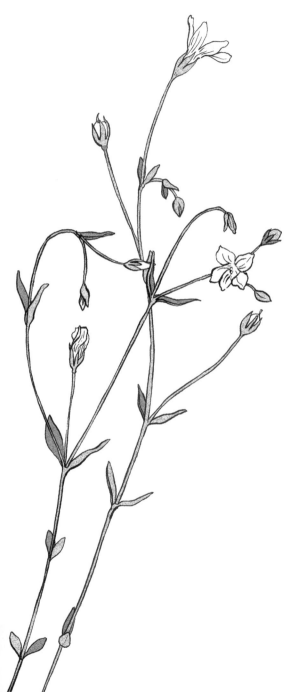

F

FAIRY FLAX
(*Linum catharticum*)

ENGLISH: Purging flax

GAELIC: *Caol miosachan / Caol-mhioschan*; *Caolach*; *Caolach-mìosa / Caolaich-mhìosa* (Colonsay); *Lion na bean sith / Lion na mna sith / Lion nam ban sith / Lìon nam Ban-sìdh* – fairy woman's flax; *Lus caolach* – slender weed or the intestinal plant; *Mionach* – bowels or intestines; *Mìosach* – medicinal or monthly

SCOTS: Laverock's lint (Lanarkshire)

The names for fairy flax are somewhat confused. It is a tiny little plant but was used as a powerful purgative – hence *catharticum* in the scientific name. It was also an abortifacient and was possibly used medicinally for menstrual issues. The two names *Mionach* and *Mìosach* may reflect these medicinal uses, but it is unclear what the context for these names is, so the monthly, or menstrual aspect may just be a mix up through the names.

FAT HEN
(*Chenopodium album* and related species)

ENGLISH: Allgood; Common frost-blite; Common white blite

GAELIC: *Bloinigean*; *Cal liath-ghlas*; *Cal liathglas* – light grey cabbage; *Càl-slapach* – flapping or splashing cabbage (Colonsay); *Praiseach brathair* – friar or monk's pot-herb; *Praiseach fhiadhain* / *Praiseach fiadhain*– wild pot-herb; *Praiseach ghlas* – green pot-herb; *Teanga mhin* – smooth tongue or mealy

SCOTS: Mails / Miles / Myles (Berwickshire); Meldweed; Melgs (Morayshire); Midden mylies (N Scotland, Selkirkshire); Midden weed; Milds; Smear docken; Smiddy leaves (Berwickshire); Wild spinage

As the Scots name 'wild spinage' suggests, fat hen is a fairly close relative of spinach, in the Amaranthaceae family. A popular foraged plant, it was an important part of the diet of poorer families. Thriving on slightly more alkaline, well-drained sites, it is often found on wasteground sandy spots, or areas with ash deposits – hence the names 'midden-weed' and 'smiddy leaves'.

Many other related species share the same names, including the robust good king Henry (*Chenopodium bonus-henricus*) and other oraches from the genera *Chenopodium* and *Atriplex*.

FERNS
(*Dryopteris* and *Polystichum* species)

Many of the large ferns are difficult to distinguish from each other and are (along with bracken) usually just named 'fern' or *raineach*. However, there are a few other specific names for some. *Marc-raineach* – horse-fern is the male fern (*Dryopteris filix-mas*); *Mearlag* – the scaly male fern (*Dryopteris affinis*); *Rain each Chaol* or *Raineach nan rodainn* – the rat's fern (Morvern, Mull and Lewis) is the narrow buckler fern (*Dryopteris carthusiana*).

The hard shield fern (*Polystichum aculeatum*) is *ibhig chruaidh*, while the soft shield fern (*Polystichum setiferum*) is *ibhig bhog*. These are both fairly modern constructed names, as many of these ferns look very similar and are difficult to distinguish, so they are mostly all treated as one thing: 'biggish ferns'. Several of the more weird and wonderful ferns or those with particular names are found throughout the rest of this book.

FERN, ROYAL
(*Osmunda regalis*)

ENGLISH: Flowering fern; Osmund-royal; Royal-bracken

GAELIC: *Raineach reangach* – from *reang* = wand or stalk; *Raineach rioghail* – royal/kingly fern; *Righ-raineach*

SCOTS: Royal brachens

The stately royal fern is uncommon but striking, so easily spotted when you come across it in its streamside habitats, and it certainly has a royal air. The orange spore-bearing tips to the fronds are superficially like flowers, but are not, so 'flowering fern' is a misnomer.

FENNEL
(Foeniculum vulgare)

GAELIC: *Fineal; Fineal-cubhraidh* – fragrant fennel; *Giùran* – bronze fennel; *Lus an t' saiodh; Lìobhag fhineil*

SCOTS: Finkil / Finkle

A popular flavouring herb long grown in Scotland, although native to southern continental Europe

FENUGREEK
(Trigonella foenum-graecum)

ENGLISH: Greek fennel

GAELIC: *Crubh-eòin; Deanntag-Ghreugach* – Greek nettle; *Fineal-Greugach* – Greek fennel; *Ionntag-Greugach* – Greek nettle

SCOTS: Cammock

This Mediterranean member of the pea family looks nothing like fennel, and the flavour is only superficially similar. Quite where the association with nettles comes from (it looks nothing like a nettle) is a job for another researcher!

FEVERFEW
(Tanacetum parthenium) – see **TANSY**

FIG
(Ficus carica)

GAELIC: *Crann fige / Crann fighis / Crann figis / Craobh fige* etc. – fig tree; *Fige / Fighis / Figis / Fiogag / Fiogais / Fioguis* – fig fruit

SCOTS: Feg (Banffshire, Aberdeenshire)

Fig is such a fundamental part of culture around the Mediterranean and Europe that, like birch or poppy, its name is similar in almost all Indo-European languages.

FIGWORT, COMMON
(*Scrophularia nodosa*)

ENGLISH: Rose noble; Stinking Roger

GAELIC: *Donn-lus / Dun lus* – brown plant, although 'dun' interpreted as a hill or height; *Farach don* – brown mallet; *Farach dubh* – black mallet; *Farum*; *Forum*; *Fothlus* – from fothlac = the horse disease known in English as glanders and *lus* = plant; *Fotlus* – crumbs, refuse, scrofulous; *Fotrum* – glandered because the roots resemble tumours; *Lus nan clugan* – cluster plant; *Lus nan cnapan* – knobbled plant; *Lus nan torranain* – thunderer's plant; *Lus-an-torranain* – from torran, an obsolete term for a little hill or knob; *Tarranan / Tarrann* – St. Ternan's herb; *Toranan / Torranan* – St. Tornan's plant; *Torrann*

This plant was long used as a treatment for scrofula, a systemic form of tuberculosis that caused swellings in the lymphatic system. It may be that the knobbly roots of the plant were seen to resemble the symptoms in humans and horses alike, so it was used medicinally under the Doctrine of Signatures, where a cure contains clues to the conditions it treats. The Gaelic names relating to the appearance of the plant make sense in this regard. However, those relating to the thunderer and St. Torran are a bit more obscure. It may relate to some connection through Taranis, Celtic god of thunder, but Carmichael's (1928) description of the plant *Torranan* does not chime at all with the appearance of *Scrophularia*, and these names may be a case of misidentification. There is certainly further work to be done here.

FLAX
(*Linum usitatissimum*)

ENGLISH: Linseed – the seed and plant

GAELIC: *Lin*; *Lion*

SCOTS: Bow; Linget; Lint; Lint-bell; Lint-boll; Lint-bow; Lint-bowe

A plant used throughout Europe, the names for flax are very similar across all Indo-European languages.

FOXGLOVE
(*Digitalis purpurea*)

GAELIC: *Caileach na mharbh* – dead lady's thimble/old wives' thimble (Staffin, Skye); *Cioch na mnatha sidheadh* – fairy's paps (South Uist, Eriskay); *Cioch nan cailleacha* – old woman's breasts (South Uist, Eriskay); *Ciochan nan cailleachan marblia* – dead old women's paps (Skye); *Cluig na mnatha sithe* – fairy woman's ear-drop; *Lus a bhalgair* – fox-weed (mid-Perthshire, Aberfeldy); *Lus an toraid* – plant of fruitfulness; *An Lus-mor*; – the big plant; *Lus-na-meala-mor*; *Lus nam Ban-sìth* – fairy woman's plant; *Meuran-a'-bhais* – thimble of death; *Meuran-na-mna-sith* – the fairy-woman's thimble; *Meuran nam caillich* – dead women's thimbles; *Meuran namn daoine marbh / Meuran nan daoine marbha* – dead men's thimbles; *Meuran nan cailleachan marbha* – the dead old woman's fingers; *Meuran-nan-cailleachan sith* – old fairy-woman's fingers; *Meuran-sith* – fairy thimble; *Sionn*

SCOTS: Dead-men's bells; Bloody bells (Lanarkshire); Bloody fingers; Bluidy bells; Bluidy-fingers; Deadmen's fingers (Inverness); Deid man's bellows (NE Scotland); Deid man's bells (NE Scotland); Fairy's thimbles (Lanarkshire); Foxter; Foxter leaves; Gensie pushon

(Orkney); King Ellwand's; Lady's/
Leddy's thummles; Leddy's thimbles;
Scotch mercury (Berwickshire); Tod's
tails (S Scotland, Roxburghshire);
Wild mercury (Berwickshire);
Witches' paps (Argyll, Ayrshire);
Witches' thimbles (Caithness,
Moray and central Scotland);
Witches' thummles (Caithness,
Moray and central Scotland)

Fascinating foxgloves are notoriously
dangerous, so many of their names
reflect this sinister reputation.
Containing the cardiac glycoside
digoxin and digitoxin, foxgloves
were used throughout Europe in
the treatment of heart conditions as
these compounds can help to regulate
heart rhythm. Although they were
effective in some cases, the very
precise dosage required probably
resulted in many fatal poisonings.
Combined with the elegant spires
of pink, finger-like flowers and their
preferred habitat of sunny banks
at woodland edges, this toxicity
evokes a feeling of otherworldly
threat redolent of the faerie folk,
so the vast majority of names relate
to the 'shidhe' (fairy folk), witches
or death. Tolkien himself explains
that 'fox-glove' is a literal carry-
over from Old English 'foxes-clofa',
and not, as is often suggested,
folks' (i.e. fairy-folks') glove.

FUMITORY
(*Fumaria* species)

GAELIC: *Dearag thalmhainn /
Dearg thalmhainn* – red earth
from *dearg* = red and *talamh* =
earth, ground; *Deathach-
thalmhainn* – from *deatach* =
smoke and *talamh* = earth, ground;
earth smoke; *Fuaim an 't siorraigh* –
the sheriff's voice, a play on the
name *Fumaria officinalis*; *Lus
deathach-thalmhainn* – the earth
smoke plant

SCOTS: Mither

The deeply dissected leaves of
these plants of wasteground are
reminiscent of smoke.

G

GARDEN PEA
(*Pisum sativum*)

GAELIC: *Peasair*; *Piseir*; *Min-pheasrach* – pea flour

SCOTS: Cob / Cod – the pod; Haistine / Hasterns / Hasting / Hastings – archaic name for early ripening varieties; Het / Hot; Huil / Pea-huil – the pod; Pea-cod – the pod; Pease strae – pea straw for fodder; Pea-shaup – the pod; Pey (NE Scotland); Pizz / Pizzer / Pizzers (NE Scotland); Shaup – the pod; Swab(s) – the pod; Swap – young pods or the peas themselves (Lothian); Whaup – young pods or the peas themselves

Peas have long been an important crop in the lowlands, with codlin varieties a particular Scottish favourite. Their protein-rich seeds and ability to nitrify the soil means they are one of the plants at the forefront of research into food security – watch this pea-shaped space!

GARLIC, WILD, AND RAMSONS
(*Allium* species – mainly *Allium ursinum*)

ENGLISH: Wild leek

GAELIC: *Creamh*; *Gairgean*; *Gairgean-garaidh*; *Garlag / Garleag*; *Goirgin garaidh*; *Lurachan*

SCOTS: Ramp / Ramps; Ramsoms (Berwickshire)

The broad-leaved flavoursome ramsons (*Allium ursinum*) are the best known and most common native garlic. Several other, narrow-leaved species have been introduced and become invasive in the lowlands – especially near rivers and streams, but are often lumped together under the same names – as garlic is garlic after all.

GARLIC MUSTARD
(*Alliaria petiolata*)

ENGLISH: Jack-by-the hedge; Sauce-alone

GAELIC: *Bo-coinneal* – cow candle; *Gabhraitheach* – rough, threatening; *Gairleach collaid* – hedge garlic

This hedgerow and roadside herb is a member of the cabbage and mustard family with a delicate garlic flavour – hence sauce-alone as it is all you could need for a flavourful sauce. Just be careful not to collect it from any area where dogs may have been peeing!

GLOBEFLOWER
(*Trollius europaeus*)

ENGLISH: Bull-jumping / Bull-jumpling (Kincardineshire); Butter-blob; Cabbage daisy; Locked daisy

GAELIC: *Leolaicheann* – drinking i.e. a goblet

SCOTS: Lapper gowan; Locker gowan; Locker gowlan; Lockety gowan; Lockin gowan; Lucken; Lucken gowan; Luggie gowan; Stocks (Borders); Witches' gowan

A plant of more southerly parts of the country, this buttercup's petals form a globe, or goblet, or a spherical box with the stamens and pistil 'locked' inside. Even the scientific name is nicely evocative – *Trollius* is said to come from 'troll'.

GOLDENROD
(*Solidago virgaurea*)

GAELIC: *Fuinneag-coille* – the wood enchantress; *Fuinseag coille*; *Slat-oir* – golden-rod

GOOSEBERRY
(*Ribes uva-crispa*)

ENGLISH: Blob; Honeyblob; Green-berry;

GAELIC: *Chrabhsag / Crobhrsag*; *Grosaid / Groiseid* – the fruit; *Preas-chrabhsag*; *Preas ghrosaid / Preas-groiseid* – gooseberry bush; *Sgeach-spionain*; *Spiontag*

SCOTS: Grosat / Groset / Grossat / Grozet / Grozzet; Grosel / Grizzle / Grozel; Grozzle / Gruzel / Gruzle Groser / Grosser; Gaskin green / Green gaskin; Hinny-blob

For one of the most love-it-or-hate-it fruits it is interesting to note the number of names this tart berry has picked up. Many of the Scots and several of the Gaelic ones are derived from the old French 'grosaid'.

GORSE
(Ulex europaeus)

ENGLISH: Whin / Furze

GAELIC: *Ait*; *Beara'ach*
(Colonsay); *Conasg* – armed (i.e.
for war); *Droighneach* – spiker;
Gunnars; *Oir*; **Onn**; *Teine*; *Uir*

SCOTS: Carline spurs / Carling
spurs / Fun / Fun bus – whin bush /
Whin-cow; Whun / Whun-bush

Two other species of gorse are found
in Scotland – *Ulex gallii* and *Ulex
minor*, but both are either very rare
or difficult to tell apart from each
other, so it may be that they are
under-recorded. Or, it may just be
that they are smaller variants of
Ulex europaeus – certainly one for
the botanists to debate...

**As *Oir*, or *Onn*, gorse represents
the letter O in the Gaelic
alphabet of tree names.**

GRASSES
(Poaceae species)

SCOTS: Bennel; Beust (SW
Scotland); Fushach / Fushloch /
Fushnach / Fuslach / (SW
Scotland); Fussock (SW Scotland);
Girse (NE Scotland) / Gorsk /
Gosk; Hose-grass; Natur girse /
Nature grass; Pile; Reesk; Sprat

This wide array of names all
applies generally to grasses, and
some beyond this as well, so 'girse'
can simply be 'plant', although
usually a herbaceous one, and is
paired with many other words to
give specific names, so butterwort
(*Pinguicula vulgaris*) is sometimes
'yirnin-girse' i.e. curdling grass
as it was used in butter and
cheesemaking.

GROUND ELDER
(*Aegopodium podagraria*)

ENGLISH: Bishop-weed; goat-weed; gout-weed

GAELIC: *Falluran*; *Lus-an-easbuig* – the Bishop's weed/plant

Ground elder may not be a gardener's favourite as it is a monster to remove when it gets in the garden, but it is edible, and was traditionally used medicinally. Introduced to Scotland around or before the mediaeval period, its use as a treatment for gout, and the fact it was grown in monastic gardens, are the main sources for its names.

GROUND IVY
(*Glechoma hederacea*)

GAELIC: *Athair lus*; *Eidheann thalmhainn* (Islay); *Iadh shlat thalmhainn* – ground ivy; *Nathair lus* – seprpent weed; *Orafoirt*; *Staoin*

SCOTS: Ground avy / Grund avy (Orkney); Ground davy / Grund davy (Orkney)

This creeping herb of woodlands has heart- or hoof-shaped leaves and was used as a flavouring for beer, hence one of its names in England – alehoof.

GROUNDSEL
(*Senecio vulgaris*)

GAELIC: *Ballan-buidhe*; *Bualan, Am* – the remedy; *Grunnasg* – perhaps from *grunnd* = ground; *Lus-phara-leith* / *Lus-phara-liath* – grey plant of St. Peter; *Sail-bhuinn* – ulcer on the heel

SCOTS: Grundsel; Gruniswallow; Grunny Swally; Swally; Wattery drums

This opportunistic, fast-cycling weed of wasteground is beautifully adapted to spread through its hundreds of seeds – 'swallowing up the ground' as it does so. This is one of many plants where the Scots names reflect their Old- or Middle-English origins.

H

HAIRY TARE
(*Ervilia hirsuta* and *Vicia hirsuta*)

GAELIC: *Cogal / Cogull* – from English cockle; *Dithean* – a name given to many small plants, including daisies; *Gall pheasair* – lentil or vetch; *Gall-peasair* – foreigner's peas; *Peasair an Arbhair* – corn peas; *Peasair luchag* (Colonsay)

SCOTS: Tares; Teer

For some reason this unfortunate species has picked up a bad reputation. It is equated with the tares of the Bible, sown on the fields of one's enemies to blight them. While it is a weed of arable land and wasteground, it actually nitrifies the soil, improving it for agriculture. However, in *cogal*, it shares a name with some of the most notoriously poisonous agricultural weeds – clearly a case of mistaken identity.

HART'S TONGUE FERN
(*Phyllitis scolopendrium*)

GAELIC: *Creamh na muice fiadhaich / Creamh mac fiadh / Creamh-mac-feidh* – wild boar's wort, or wild boar's garlic; *Teang' an fèidh / Teanga an fhèidh* – hart's tongue

The simple fronds of hart's tongue are unmistakeable, with their parallel rows of sporangia on the undersides. The base of the plant's rhizome was one of several fern-derived medicines used to kill intestinal worms.

HAWTHORN

ENGLISH: Dead man's flourish;
Flourish

GAELIC: *Ban-sgitheach* –
whitethorn; *Droigheann*;
Droigheann geal; *Fearra-dhris*;
Huath; *Sgeach* – the fruits;
Sgeach-chaor; *Sgiteach* / *Sgìtheach*
Sgitheag / *Sgithich*; *Sgitheach*
geal – white thorn; **Uath**; *Uir*

SCOTS: Boojuns – the fruits
(Invernesshire); Breid-an-cheese /
Cheese-an-breid; Chaw; Fleerish /
Flourish; Hathorn / Hathorne /
Hawthorne; Has tree (S Scotland);
Haw; Haw-berry; Haw-bush /
Haw-buss (Dumfriesshire,
Selkirkshire); Haw-stone;
Haw-tree; Lady's meat – of the
edible leaves and young buds
(Caithness; Kirkcudbrightshire)

Hawthorn is a widespread tree of
hedgerows and broadleaved woodland
that has adopted a great many
names over the centuries – with
different parts of the plant picking
up individual names. 'Flourish' and
related terms refer to the flowerheads
while the haws are the fruit, so
a distinction is made for the haw
tree or haw bush itself. Haws were
eaten in the past and are still made
into jellies and jams on a small
scale. The wood was an important
fuel and hawthorns are one of the
main species dressed with cloths as
clootie trees to draw the attention
of local spirits, faerie folk or saints.

**Hawthorn represents the
letter U as *Uath* in the Gaelic
alphabet of tree names.**

HAZEL
(Corylus avellana)

GAELIC: *Alltuinn; Cailtin / Calldain / Calldainn / Callduin / Calltainn / Calltuinn; Caitlin; Caomhan; Coill;* **Coll;** *Colluinn; Crann-calltainn* – hazel tree; *Craobh-challtain / Craobh-challtainn* – shoot or stick

SCOTS: Crack nut / Cracker nut – the nut of the plant; Haissel / Hasill / Haslie / Hassel / Hassil – mostly referring the nut; Hassly / Hasslie / Hazellie – abounding with hazel; Scob / Scub – twig as used for thatching; St. John's nut – a double nut

It is no surprise the hazel has picked up such an array of names. It is a tree of huge practical value and much vaunted in folklore. Almost all of the ancient hazel stands in Scotland were managed by coppicing, producing nutritious, storable nuts, stems for charcoal and fencing as well as bark for tanning. Twigs were used for divining, and the nuts were seen as a symbol of knowledge, but the plant was sometimes considered unlucky.

Hazel represents the letter C as *Coll* in the Gaelic alphabet of tree names.

HEATH RUSH
(Juncus squarrosus) – see **RUSH,** HEATH

HEATH, CROSS-LEAVED
(Erica tetralix)

ENGLISH: Bog heather

GAELIC: *Fraoch an ruinnse* – rinsing heather; *Fraoch Frangach* – French heather; *Fraoch gucanach* (Colonsay); *Fraoch meangain* – branched heath; *Mion-fraoch*

SCOTS: Heather birns

The cross-leaved heath is typical of slightly drier, sandier areas than the other two common species of heather, in spite of its name of bog-heather.

HEATHER, BELL
(*Erica cinerea*)

ENGLISH: Heather-bell; She-heather

GAELIC: *Fraoch bhadhain* – tufted heath; *Biadh na ciree fraoich* – grouse-food; *Dluth-fraoch, Fraoch a' bhadain* – tufted heather; *Fraoch an dearrasain* – rustling or buzzing heath; *Fraoch barr-guc*; *Fraoch dearg* – red heather; *Fraoch meangain*; *Fraoch sgriachain* – screeching heath; *Fraoch speadanach* – crackling heath; *Pubal beannach* – angled tent

SCOTS: Carlin heather / Carline heather

The smaller stature and slender leaves of this species perhaps give it the name 'she-heather' in contrast to the scaly leaves and larger, shrubby habit of *Calluna vulgaris* – the 'he-heather'.

HEATHER, LING
(*Calluna vulgaris*)

ENGLISH: Common heather; Dog heather; He-heather

GAELIC: *Fraoch*; *Ur*

SCOTS: Hadder / Hather / Hedder / Hether; Hadry; Heather-cow; Heather-cowe / Hen's ware

The near-ubiquitous heather of the uplands, this species defines a huge portion of Scotland's landscape. It is an important food for young grouse, and managed for them, as well as being resistant to deer-grazing, so it is a self-maintaining, if somewhat biodiversity-poor ecosystem in its own right. That said, it made an incredibly tough thatching material and source of *sugen* – stout heather ropes.

As *Ur*, Ling heather represents the letter U in the Gaelic alphabet of tree names.

HEMLOCK
(*Conium maculatum*)

GAELIC: *Boinne-mear*; *Cornan-fail* – the little fatal cup; *Curran cruaidh*; *Detheodha Eiteodha* / *Iteodha* / *Iteotha* – the feathered plant; *Minbhar* / *Min-bharr Minmhear* / *Minmheur* – soft-topped/soft-leaved; *Mongach mhear* / *Mungach-mear* – the smooth glossy mane; *Munmhear* / *Muinmhear* / *Muinmheur*; *Ti-theodha* (South Uist, Eriskay)

SCOTS: Bunnel; Coo-cakes; Hech-How; Humlock; Humly; Humly rose; Kaka; Kex, Scab

Many of the Gaelic names for Hemlock are deceptively pleasant, although *cornan-fail* is a blunt reference to the fateful draught of hemlock that killed Socrates. It is very much a plant of south and eastern lowlands and, to a lesser extent, the islands. The related hemlock water dropwort (*Oenanthe crocata*) is a more western plant – common throughout lower areas of the north and the islands, so there may be some overlap in names, although they are distinct. Hemlock likes drier areas, is taller and more slender with steely grey foliage, red spots and a smell of mouse-piss, whereas Hemlock water dropwort has a sickly sweet stench and looks like nothing so much as a large, evil celery, lurking by the waterside – both are magnificent plants. Hemlock water-dropwort's names in Gaelic are *aiteodha* on Colonsay, *dàtha bàn iteodha* or *tàthabha*, although the best is *fealladh bog* – sometimes translated as 'gentle deceit'.

HEMP
(*Cannabis sativa*)

GAELIC: *Cainb* / *Caineab*; *Corcach*

SCOTS: Hempt; Kempit

Cultivated in the past for its fibre, and in modern times as an illicit or medicinal drug, this species probably has more names than any other in this book, although few if any are particularly Scottish.

HENBANE
(*Hyoscyamus niger*)

GAELIC: *Caoch-nan-cearc* – that which blinds hens; *Caothach-nan-cearc* – that which maddens hens; *Crann-gafainn* – the dangerous tree; *Deo*; *Deodha Detheodha / Detheogha / Di-theodha* – breath, that which is destructive of life; *Fegan*; *Gabhann / Gafann* – the dangerous one

A non-native and fairly rare plant found only around warm coastal areas. It was an important soporific medicine, though, so has garnered several names in Gaelic.

HERB-PARIS
(*Paris quadrifolia*)

GAELIC: *Aon-dhearc*

SCOTS: Deil in a bush (Aberdeenshire, Perthshire); Glamourie-berrie; True-love (Dumfriesshire)

'Deil in a bush' is usually Nigella (*Nigella damascena*) or sometimes carrot (*Daucus carota*), as these two species have many bracts surrounding the fruit. Herb-Paris is similar in having a ruff of stamens and four leaves surrounding the fruit inside – a plump, black berry – nicely reflected in the Gaelic name.

HERB-ROBERT
(*Geranium robertianum*)

ENGLISH: Cancer-wort

GAELIC: *Earball-righ*; *Luibh-na-maclan*; *Lus ros / Lus-rois* – rose-wort, plant; *Reilteag* – starlet; *Rial chuil* – that which rules insects; *Rian roighe* – crane's bill; *Righeal cuil* – reprover/repeller of flies; *Righeal righ* – reprover/repeller of kings; *Ruideal* – red-haired

SCOTS: Stinking Billy

This common geranium, or cranesbill of woods and wasteground has a strong smell a bit like burning rubber, said to keep away flies and other insects. Its efficacy on kings has probably not been tested, but is almost certainly a reflection of some sectarian sentiment of days gone by.

HOGWEED
(*Heracleum sphondylium*)

ENGLISH: Cow parsnip

GAELIC: *Fiuran*; *Giuran* (Colonsay); *Gunnachan sputachain* – squirt guns; *Meacan-a'-chruidh* – cow's plant; *Odharan* – pale, dun, yellowish

SCOTS: Bear skeiters – barley-shooters; Bunnen; Bunewand / Bunwand; Buneweed; Bunnel; Bunnen; Bunnert; Bunnerts; Bunnle; Bunwort; Coo-cakes; Cow-Keeks; Cowkeep (Fife); Cow parsnip; Dead man's forest / Deid men's forest; Hemlock; Kecksi / Keksi / Kex (Shetland)

This robust member of the carrot family is found throughout Scotland, especially in lower altitude grasslands. Easily identified, the plant was an important food for livestock and the hollow stem was used as a popgun, water-pistol or a pea-shooter for barley and other grains. But it must be treated with caution – although not so bad as its giant cousin *Heracleum mantegazzianum*, the psoralen-rich sap reacts with sunlight to cause blisters and burns on the skin, which may well be the source of some of its more sinister names, associating it with hemlock. Parsnip (*Pastinaca sativa*) is a similar looking, close relative and its sap can also cause mild blisters in the sunshine. These similarities may be the source of the name cow parsnip, and be contrasted with the more delicate and distantly related cow parsley (*Anthriscus sylvestris*). The most evocative name, though, must be 'deid men's forest' – a haunting description of the dead, grey, spindly stems in winter.

HOLLY
(*Ilex aquifolium*)

GAELIC: *Chuillin / Cuileann / Cuilionn / Cuillean* – the defender, from *cul* = defence or *cuil* = that which prohibits; *Cran-cuilinn / Crann-cuilinn*; *Craobh-chuilinn* – holly tree; *Cuilionn-breac* – speckled defender

SCOTS: Holine / Holing / Hollin

One of the most instantly identifiable trees in the Scottish flora, and one known by almost everyone. It has garnered a few names, with the Gaelic ones being more descriptive.

HONEYSUCKLE
(*Lonicera periclymenum*)

ENGLISH: Bindweed; Lady's fingers; Woodbind

GAELIC: *Baine-ghamhnaich / Bainne-ghamhnaich* – the yearling's milk; *Caora mhea lain*; *Caora mhea nglain*; *Cas-fa-chrann* – that which twists around trees; *Dealbh a'chrainn*; *Deoghalag*; *Deolag / Deothlag / Deothlagan*; *Duilliur-feithlean(n)* – leaf (and) sinew; *Eidheann-mu-chrann* – plant that twists around a tree; *Faileantan*; *Feathlog fa chrann Feileag*; *Feith / Feithlean / Feithleann* – sinew or tendon, of the stem; *Ladh slat / Iadh shlat* – the twig that surrounds; *Ladhlainn*; *Leum-a'-chrann* – leaps between trees; *Lus na meala* – honey plant; *Uillean / uilleann*

SCOTS: Binweed; Binwud; Hinnysickle; Leddy's fingers

Lady's or 'leddy's fingers' are the long, delicate flowers. Coupled with the heady scent of the flowers and the twining growth habit up the trunks of trees, it's easy to see how this plant developed such swathes of romantic names. The berries are inedible so perhaps they do not feature in names as much as would be expected from their luminous red, jewel-like hue.

HORSETAILS
(*Equisetum* species)

ENGLISH: Dutch rushes; Scouring rush

GAELIC: *Cuilg-sruth-eich* – flowing horse's tail; *Cuiridin*; *Earball an eich* / *Earball-eich* / *Earbuill-Each* – horse's tail; *Earbull capuill* – colt's or pony's tail (Colonsay). Species from wet areas may be *Clois* or *Clo-uisge*

SCOTS: Deil's rattles; Paddock pipes / Paddy pipes / Puddock pipes – frog or toad's pipes

Although these are a diverse group of plants for the botanist, the horsetails do look superficially similar, so the vast majority of species share the same common names without distinction. Individual names have been 'invented' in recent names to match with the species as recognised by science, so the Great horsetail (*Equisetum telmateia*), for example is known simply as *Earball an eich Mòr*. This is a particularly robust and attractive species from wet woodlands. Horsetails were traditionally used for scouring pans as they contain coarse silica granules. The best species for this was *Equisetum hyemale*, known in Gaelic as *Cuiridin garbh* – the rough horsetail.

HOUSE-LEEK
(*Sempervivum tectorum*)

ENGLISH: Healing blade / healing leaf

GAELIC: *Creamh-garaidh* / *creamh-garraidh* – garden garlic; *Lus gharaidh* – garden plant; *Lus nan cluas* – ear plant; *Norn*; *Norp*; *Oirp* – from French 'orpine'; *Tin gealach* / *Tineas na gealaich* – moon-sick or lunatic; *Tirpin* / *Tirpean* – ground pine (although Irish Gaelic); *Toir pin*

SCOTS: Fews / Foos, Foose / Fouets / Fuets – perhaps from Saxon *Fegan*, 'to clean'; Fow / Fows; Hockerie-topner; Hoos; Sengreen – ever green

The juice from the dense, succulent rosettes of house-leek were used as a soothing treatment for wounds, and the whole plant is one of several similar succulents that were believed to protect the house on which they grew from lightning strikes.

I

IODINE KELP
— see **KELPS**

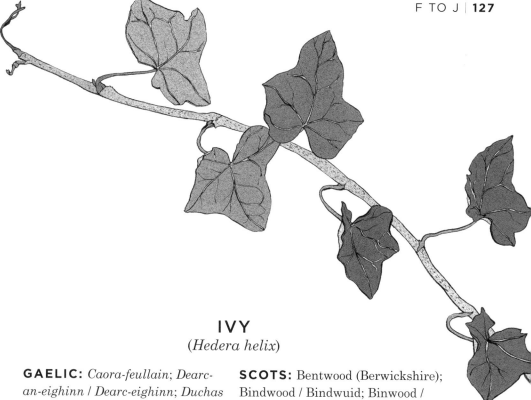

IVY
(*Hedera helix*)

GAELIC: *Caora-feullain*; *Dearc-an-eighinn* / *Dearc-eighinn*; *Duchas* (Colonsay); *Eidheann* – that which clothes or covers/covering (Arran); *Eidheann mu chrann*; *Eidheannach* (Argyll, Arran); *Eidheann-mu-chrann* – that which clothes around the tree; *Eidheantach* (Arran); *Eidhionn*; *Eidhionn-na-creige* – ivy of the rock; *Eidhne*; *Eidhnean* – that which clothes or covers; *Eigheann* – possibly from *eigh* = a web; *Faighleadh*; *Gath* – covering; *Gath, An* – the spear or dart; **Gort** – sour, bitter perhaps of the berries; *Ladh-shlat* – the twig that surrounds; *Lallan* / *Ialuinn* – that which surrounds, possibly referring to *helix*

SCOTS: Bentwood (Berwickshire); Bindwood / Bindwuid; Binwood / Binwuid; Eevie; Ivery; Ivin

Almost all the names of ivy make sense from its distinctive habit – clothing or binding trees in its growth, or the berries. **Ivy is G – Gort in the Gaelic alphabet of tree names.**

J

JUNIPER
(*Juniperus communis*)

GAELIC: *Aiteal* / *Aiteil* / *Aitiol*;
Aiteann / *Aiten* / *Aitinn* / *Aitionn* /
Aittin; *Aitnach* (Bannfshire,
Morayshire); *Becora-leacra*; *Bior-
leacain* – perhaps from *bior* = sharp,
of the needles and *leacann* = broad
side of a hill; *Caora staoin* / *Caorainn-
staoine* – the berry-like cone, *staoin*
is a little drinking cup; *Dearc aiten* /
Dearc-aitinn – juniper 'berry' or cone;
Iubhar – yew; *Iubhar-beinne* – hill-
yew; *Iubhar-chreige* – rock-yew;
Iubhar-thalmhainn – ground-yew;
Lus-na-staoine – plant of the little
drinking cup; *Samh*; *Sineubhar*;
Staoin – little drinking cup

SCOTS: Aiten; Aitnach (Banffshire,
Morayshire); Eaten; Eatin-berries;
Etnach (NE Scotland); Etnagh
berries; Jenepere (Aberdeenshire
and NE Scotland); Melmet; Melmot /
Melmot berries / Melmont berries
(Morayshire); Savin

Unmistakeable and important as a smokeless fuel, flavouring for liquors and food, as well as an abortifacient, juniper has picked up an array of names. This versatility led to its overexploitation, and coupled with damage to the ancient scrublands by livestock, it was under significant threat. Thankfully, this wonderful little conifer is making a recovery, aided by widespread conservation efforts. In older Scots, 'savin' was perhaps the most widely used name for juniper, although this probably derives from the continental European species *Juniperus sabina* – the cones of which are poisonous. Juniper is one of several plants where the Gaelic names have been adopted into Scots as well.

K to N

K

KALE
(Brassica oleracea) – please see **CABBAGE**

KELPS
(*Laminaria* species and
Sacchorhiza polyschides)

ENGLISH: Oarweed; Sea girdles
(Orkney)

GAELIC: *Barr-dearg* (Skye, Unst);
Barr-roc; *Barr-staimh / Barr-stamh*;
Bragaire, Am / Braggir – the frond
(lamina); *Bruca dubh* (South Uist,
Eriskay); *Carraig*; *Ceilp*; *Dalanach /
Dallanach*; *Doire / Doirean* (Islay,
Lismore, Skye); *Druidhean* –
of the stipe (stem); *Dubh-stamh* –
black kelp; *Duitheaman* (Tiree);
Langadal; *Leathagan*; *Liadhag* –
of the frond (lamina); *Luath
feamnach*; *Ramasg*; *Rioflais*; *Roc*;
Sgliugan; *Slat mhara* – sea wand;
Stamh; *Tobhar dearg*

SCOTS: Red ware (Orkney)
Tangle / Tangles; Slattyvarie
(Argyll)

These incredible organisms are the
most robust seaweeds in Scottish
waters, coping with storm and tide
and all the while enduring armies
of grazing shellfish, and sheltering
young fish among their fronds.
Two main species make up the
heart of the huge kelp forests
off the rocky shores, *Laminaria
digitata* and *Laminaria hyperborea*.
The first of these has a more
slender, bendier stem (called a

stipe in seaweeds), so can cope with being partially out of the water, bending over without snapping. This means it is generally found higher up the shore, where the lowest tides will leave it a little exposed. *Laminaria hyperborea* is stouter, and found a bit deeper, along with a third kelp, the huge and alien-looking furbelows (*Sacchoriza polyschides*) which is known in Gaelic as *sgrothach*. All of these were an important source of fertiliser, and still are on a small scale, although the wracks (*Fucus* species) which live higher up the shore are more easily obtained. The long, stem-like stipe and knobbly holdfast of *Laminaria hyperborea*, the deeper-water species, made an ideal swingel – the head-part of a threshing flail. You might notice we are not using a common name for these species – partly because the common names for seaweeds are often a mess, with many lumped in together under such names as kelp or tangles. Even the term 'kelp' can often mean any chunky brown seaweed - including the wracks and even species from across the globe such as the N American Bull Kelp (*Macrocystis pyrifera*, pictured here) Although we geeky botanists and phycologists are never one to impose on others, this is clearly a good example where the scientific names help avoid ambiguity. That said, *Laminaria digitata* is often referred to as oarweed.

KIDNEY VETCH
(*Anthyllis vulneraria*)

ENGLISH: Ladies' fingers / Lady's fingers (Lanarkshire)

GAELIC: *Cas an uain* – Lamb's foot; *Dithean carrach* / *Meoir Mhuire* – Mary's fingers

SCOTS: Dog's paise (Banffshire)

The fluffy woollen flower-heads of this little member of the pea family were used to treat open wounds as a vulnerary – absorbing blood and pus. This is the root of the species' scientific epithet.

KNAPWEED
(*Centaurea nigra*)

ENGLISH: Black knapweed; Hard-head; Lesser knapweed

GAELIC: *Capan dubh* / *Cnapan dubh* – the black knob; *Mullach dubh* – black top; *Seamrag-nan-each* – horse's clover (Colonsay)

SCOTS: Hard heid (Kirkcudbrightshire, but used widely); Horse-knot; Tassel – perhaps from a vague similarity to teasel, or it is somewhat tassel-like (Berwickshire)

The hard, black heads of knapweed are very distinctive with their thistle-like tuft of flowers growing from the top, so it is perhaps no surprise that almost all the names relate to this simple descriptive point – the only exception is *Seamrag-nan-each* – horse's shamrock or clover, as it is perhaps a bit of a stretch to suggest they look very clover-like.

KNOTGRASS
(*Polygonum aviculare*)

ENGLISH: Egg wrack; Knobbled seaweed

GAELIC: *Builgach* – a sack; *Feamainn bhalgainn* / *Feamainn bholgainn* – tangled or knotted; *Feamainn bholgainn*; *Feamainn bhuidhe* – yellow seaweed; *Feamainn-cheilp*; *Gleadhrach*

SCOTS: Yellow tang

Often misnamed bladder wrack, this chunky seaweed has large, single air bladders rather than the smaller, usually paired bladders of bladder wrack (*Fucus vesiculosus*). Like many of the larger brown seaweeds, it comes under the name tang or tangles. This species was extremely important as a fertiliser.

L

LADY FERN
(*Athyrium filix-foemina*)

ENGLISH: Lady bracken

GAELIC: *Raineach Mhuire / Raineach Moire* – Mary's fern

SCOTS: Leddy bracken; Leddy fern

These names all reflect how this fern was seen as more feminine than the similar, but more robust, male fern (*Dryopteris filix-mas*).

LADY'S BEDSTRAW
(*Galium verum*)

ENGLISH: Lady's bed; Yellow bedstraw; Yellow ladies' bedstraw

GAELIC: *Bun na ruamh*; *Leabadh ban rith*; *Leabadh ban sith* – fairy woman's bed; *Lus an leasaich* – the rennet herb (Glen Lyon); *Luibh Chu-chulainn*; *Lus Chuchulainn* – Cu-chullainn's herb; *Màdar fraoich* – heather madder; *Ruadh / Ruadhain / Ruamh / Ruin* – reddish

SCOTS: Keeslip; Leddy's beds

This versatile plant was used as a filler for mattresses, as the name suggests, but was also a source of red dye like the related madder (*Rubia tinctoria*) and a rennet – as Lightfoot (1777) records: 'The rennet is made with a decoction of this herb. The Highlrs commonly added the leave of *Urtica dioica* ... With a little salt'. Over-collection threatened both the plant and the sandy habitats on which it often grows.

LADY'S MANTLE, ALPINE
(*Alchemilla alpina*)

GAELIC: *Cota* – coat; *Cota preasach nighinn an righ*; *Falluing* – mantle; *Meangan Moire*; *Meangan Muire* – Virgin Mary's twig; *Miann Moire* – Mary's desire/delight; *Miann Muire*; *trusgan* – a cloak or mantle; *Feurr carrach* – a recent name

A delicate little *Alchemilla* with silvery undersides to the leaves.

LAVENDER
(*Lavandula angustifolia* and other species)

GAELIC: *Lothail / Lothair*; *Lus liath, An* – the grey plant; *Lus-na-tuise* – incense plant

SCOTS: Lauender; Lavendar; Lavenderris; Leavender

The Scots names and spellings for this Mediterranean plant are all archaic, so it was certainly introduced and being grown in Scotland by the 14th century. Lavender water is *uisge-an-lothair*.

LAVER
(*Porphyra umbilicalis*)

GAELIC: *Slabhagan Slabhcan* (South Uist); *Slabhcean* (Lewis); *Slochdan Sloucan*

SCOTS: Slaak / Slake / Slauk / Slawk / Slock / Slokan / Sloke

Laver is a delicate edible seaweed that was commonly collected and widely eaten – indeed, it often came with fish from the fishmonger. The river Forth's Sloke Rocks and Laverrockbank are two of many localities where it was collected around the coast. It was the key ingredient in 'marine sauce'. The Scots names were also more generally applied to algae – especially if it was slimy and a nuisance.

LEMON-SCENTED FERN
(*Oreopteris limbosperma*)

ENGLISH: Mountain fern / Sweet mountain fern

GAELIC: *Creidhm-raineach* / *Crim-raineach* (Colonsay) / *Faile-raineach* / *Failte raineach* – scented or welcome fern; *Raineach an Fhàile* – sweet fern

LETTUCE
(*Lactuca sativa*)

GAELIC: *Liatas*; *Liatus*; *Luibhe-inithe* – edible plant

SCOTS: Laituce

The name 'lettuce' and most of the names here derive from *Lactuca* – the milk-plant, as early cultivars of lettuce and wild lettuces had milky sap.

LORDS AND LADIES
(*Arum maculatum*)

ENGLISH: Cuckoo pint; Wake-robin

GAELIC: *Cluas chaoin* – soft ear; *Cuthaidh* – head or possibly bulb; *Gachar*; *Gaoicin cuthigh*

SCOTS: Aron

A common plant of shady woodlands in the lowlands.

LOUSEWORTS
(*Pedicularis* species)

ENGLISH: Cock's comb; Deadmen's bellows; Honeysookies

GAELIC: *Bainne-bo-gamhnach*; *Bainne-crodh-laoigh*; *Bainne ghabhair / Bainne ghabhar* – goat's milk; *Bainne ghamhnaich / Bainne nam gamhna* – yearling's or bullock's milk (South Uist, Eriskay); *Lus grolla* – the cricket's plant; *Lus na mail / Lus nam mail* – louse plant; *Lus na meala* – honey plant; *Lus riabach* – the brindled plant, or possibly the Devil's plant; *Lus riabhach monaidh* – the brindled or Devil's plant of the mountain; *Milsean-monaidh* – sweet mountain-plant; *Modhalan dearg* – red modest one, *modhalan* is a name for the related yellow rattle (*Rhinanthus minor*)

SCOTS: Bee-sookies; Deidmen's bellows; Hinney-flooer; Honeysookies; Sookies

These hemiparasitic plants are found in wet habitats and are striking with their pink petals and intricately feathered leaves, so have inevitably accrued some interesting names. The two main species are lousewort (*Pedicularis sylvatica*) and the larger marsh lousewort or red rattle (*Pedicularis palustris*). The flowers of lousewort are a good source of nectar for both bees and those needing a sugar hit while out on the hills.

One belief was that goats feeding on the plant would yield more milk. The Gaelic *bainne ghamhnaich* is a little unclear, as yearling bullocks produce no milk, although one interpretation is sperm, rather than milk, so implying the bullocks would be more fertile. On the flip side, the English common name and the Gaelic *lus na mail* may come from a belief that sheep feeding on the plant would become louse-riddled. But, of course, there are counter-tales of the plant being used to combat lice infestations!

LOVAGE, SCOTS
(*Ligusticum scoticum*) – see SCOTS LOVAGE

M

MAIDENHAIRS
(*Adiantum capillus-veneris*
and *Asplenium trichomanes*)

ENGLISH: The virgin's hair –
Maidenhair spleenwort (*Adiantum capillus-veneris*); Black spleenwort or common maidenhair is
Asplenium trichomanes

GAELIC: *Failtean fionn* is either species, while the following are
Asplenium trichomanes:
Dubh-chosach – dark-stemmed;
Failtean fionn – resplendent, fair;
Lus a chorrain; *Lus na seilg /
Lus na seilge* – spleen plant;
Lus-a'-chorrain – herb of the scythe;
Urthalmahan – green of the earth

Maidenhair spleenwort (*Asplenium trichomanes*) is a delicate little fern found growing on the mortar in walls throughout Scotland – as in everywhere. Its fronds consist of a wiry black stem (the rachis) holding the leaflet-like pinnules together in a long, feathery structure a little reminiscent of a pancreas (rather than a spleen). Maidenhair fern is much rarer, known in only a couple of places this far north in Scotland. It is more elaborately branched, but fundamentally similar. The English and scientific names are both a bit scurrilous – alluding to pubic hair.

MALLOWS
(*Malva* species)

GAELIC: *Crubh-chunnbhadh*;
Grobais; *Lus mor* – big plant;
Lus na meala mor – abundant
honey; *Lus nam meall mòra* – plant
of the big clusters; *Mil-mheacan* –
honey plant; *Socas*; *Trom-bhod* –
heavy tail; *Ucas fheadhair / Ucas
fiadhain* – wild mallow

SCOTS: Biscuities; Cheesies;
Maws

The Scots names, like those for
several species of unrelated thistles,
come from the edible receptacle at
the base of the fruit, which has a
texture a bit like cheddar cheese.

MAPLE, FIELD
(*Acer campestre*)

GAELIC: *Crann malpais /
Crann mhailp / Craobh mhailp /
Craobh Mhalpais* and variants –
satchel tree

These Gaelic names derive from the
shape of the fruits – a large, winged
specimen which is dispersed by the
wind. For a little more information
on maples, see the entry under
sycamore (*Acer pseudoplatanus*).

MARIGOLD

(Glebionis / Chrysanthemum segetum and *Calendula* species)

ENGLISH: Marigold

GAELIC: *Bhile-bhuide, A / Bile bhuidhe* – yellow blossom; *Bileach choigreach* – stranger or foreigner; *Buildheag-an-t-samhraidh* – 'summer yellow' usually used for buttercups; *Cluaran* – usually used for thistles; *Dithean* – generic term for daisy-like plants; *Dithean-bhuidhe / Dithean-oir*; *Eointeann duidhe* (South Uist, Eriskay); *Grualan* (Lochalsh); *Liathan*; *Lus-Mhairi* – Mary's plant; *Neoinean*; *Paidirean* (Argyllshire)

SCOTS: Gool / Goul / Gule; Guild / Guilde; Manelet; Yellow gowan

Corn marigold (*Glebionis segetum* or *Chrysanthemum segetum*) and the much less common field marigold (*Calendula arvensis*) are the classic golden marigolds traditionally seen as weeds of cornfields, but many of the names here apply equally across garden marigolds and related species in the daisy family.

MARRAM GRASS
(*Ammophila arenaria*)

ENGLISH: Sea marram; Matweed

GAELIC: *Meilearach / Milearach / Mileurach / Milreach* – from the Norse *melr* = bent grass; *Mileair*; *Muirineach* – ocean, or ocean's bounty; *Muran*

Marram grass is one of the two large species of grass that bind sand dunes together – the other is lyme grass (*Leymus arenarius*), which has far broader leaves with a steely blue sheen. The two are often confused – not so much for identification, but the names are muddled up, as marram is the more famous of the two and is often applied to the *Leymus*, but the true marram has tightly rolled green leaves. Both were used to weave basketry and mats – particularly in areas where other plants were scarce – hence the English 'matweed'.

MARSH-CINQUEFOIL
(*Potentilla palustris*)

GAELIC: *Cno-leana* – bog nut; *Còig-bhileach Uisge* – five-leaved water-plant; *Coigsheag* – water-fives; *Maonag*

A distinctive water plant with five palmately arranged leaflets to each leaf.

MARSH MARIGOLD
(*Caltha palustris*)

ENGLISH: Kingcup (Lanarkshire, and more widely in Britain)

GAELIC: *Bearnan-bealltainn* – Beltane or May-day plant; *Brog an eich uisge* – water horse's shoes; *A' Carrach-shod*; *Chorrach shod* – clumsy one of the marsh; *A' Chorra-fhod* – heron of the peat or turf, perhaps misrecorded by Lightfoot (1777); *Dithean buidhe bealltainn* (South Uist, Eriskay); *Lus buidhe bealltainn*; *Lus Muire / Lus-Mairi* – Mary's plant; *Plubairsin*

SCOTS: Blogda / Bludda / Blugga – horse's hooves (Shetland); Fiddle; Gollan / Golland / Gowan (Banffshire, Caithness); Horse-gowan; Jonette – from French *Jaunette*, 'little yellow'; Lapper gowan; Water golland / Water gowland (S Scotland); Wildfire (Kirkcudbrightshire); Yellow gollan / Yellow gowan / Yellow gowlan (N Scotland)

A striking water plant with large yellow flowers. It was relatively little used traditionally, but its cheerful appearance and ease of identification may be responsible for the many names it has adopted.

MEADOWSWEET
(*Filipendula ulmaria*)

ENGLISH: Cu-Chullain's belt; Lady of the meadow; Queen of the meadow; Meadow queen

GAELIC: *Airgead-luachra* / *Airgiod luachra* – silvery rush; *Chrois cu-chulainn* / *Cneas chù chulainn*; *Cneas chuchlainn* / *Crios chu-chlainn* / *Cneas chùchulainn* / *Rios Chuchulainn* – waist-belt of Cu-chullain; *Luibh-a'-cneas* – plant of the waist; *Luibhean dìolan* – little bastard herb; *Lus-nan-gillean-oga*

SCOTS: Blakin-Girse – Blacking plant (Shetland); Deid man's flourish; Lady o meadow / Lady of the meadow / Leddy o'meadow / Leddy o' the meadow; Meduart / Medwort – mead-plant; Queen o' the meadow; Yirnin girse (Shetland); Yolgirse (Shetland)

As well as acting as a painkiller, meadowsweet was used to flavour mead and other drinks, which is where it gets its name from – it's just convenient coincidence that it grows in wet meadows. Some of these meadow-related names are shared with the superficially similar cow parsley (*Anthriscus sylvestris*), while 'blakin girse' is shared with other tannin-rich plants of wet areas used to make black inks and dyes.

The Gaelic references to *Cuchullain* allude to its supposed use in a potion or bath said to calm the Irish hero down after his battle-fury. The reference to this attractive plant as *Luibhean dìolan* may be one of these intriguing suggestions of plants that can easily be picked as a posy by one intent on wooing a maiden – a kind of sleazy impromptu gift.

MELANCHOLY THISTLE
(*Cirsium heterophyllum*) – see **THISTLE**

MERMAID'S TRESSES
(*Chorda filum*)

ENGLISH: Cat gut; Dead man's ropes; Sea lace

GAELIC: *Driamlach / Driamlaichean* – a fishing line; *Gille Mu leann / Gille-mu-lunn* – young man's net; *Langadar / Langadair* – the longest one

SCOTS: Luckie's lines; Lucky-Minny's lines (Shetland)

An unmistakeable seaweed – its unbranched, dark brown strands reach more than three metres in length and are covered with extremely fine slimy hairs that give it a strange aura underwater. Coupled with its undulating movements in the swell, it really could be mermaid's hair. Reasonably tough, it was used to make nets, hence some of the names.

MILFOIL, ALTERNATE-LEAVED WATER
(*Myriophyllum alternifolium*)

GAELIC: *Cair-thalmhainn* – ground spark; *Lus-chosghad-na-fola* – plant that stanches bleeding; *Lus-na-fola* – blood weed; *Snaithe baitei / Snaithe-bathta / Snàthainn bhàthaidh / Snàthe bhàthaidh* – drowned or drowning thread

The first three Gaelic names here are more commonly applied to yarrow (*Achillea millefolium*), another plant that is often referred to as a milfoil, although the two are unrelated. Milfoil's large number of thread-like leaves are slightly similar to the very finely dissected leaves of yar.

MILKWORTS
(*Polygala* species)

GAELIC: *Claideamh a' choilich dhuibh*; *Glùineach* – with many joints; *Lus a bhaine* – milk plant; *Siabann nam Ban-sìdh / Siabunnnam-ban-sith* – fairy woman's soap (Colonsay)

This dainty little plant of moorlands was widely believed to increase milk yields.

MINTS
(*Mentha* species)

GAELIC: *Cartal*; *Cartal-uisge* – water mint; *Mionnt*; *Meannt* / *Meanntas* / *Mionntas*; *Miontt choille* – wood mint (*Mentha longifolia*); *Meannt an uisge* – water mint; *Mionnt gharaidh* – garden mint; *Miontt each* – horse mint (*Mentha longifolia*); *Miontt fiadhan* – wild mint; *Miunn*; *Piunnt*

In Gaelic and Scots, the many varieties of mint are distinguished as they are in English, but fundamentally the name *mentha* and variants are universal across Europe – hence *mionnt* and mint.

MISTLETOE
(*Viscum album*)

GAELIC: *Druidh-lus* / *Druidhe-lus* – Druids plant; *Sùgh an daraich* – sap of the oak; *Uile-ice* / *Uil'-ioc* – all-heal of panacea

SCOTS: Misle

Although rare in Scotland, except for in the south, mistletoe has garnered a range of names in Gaelic in particular. These are more likely to be fairly recent or artificial inventions based on classical Roman accounts of the importance of the plant rather than its use in northern Druidical tradition. That said, trade routes were extensive from the Bronze Age, and commodities such as mistletoe may readily have been moved throughout Europe.

MOONWORT
(Botrychium lunaria)

ENGLISH: Moon-fern / Moon-fern leaf

GAELIC: *Dealt-lus / Deur-lus* – dew or drizzle plant; *Luan lus* – moonwort; *Lus nam Mìos* – monthly wort

SCOTS: Meenwort and other variant spellings

The tiny fronds of moonwort are a rare sight in their grassland habitats, but the wavy edges to the frond look somewhat like little crescent moons, which may be a source of the names, although it may also be the belief that this magical little plant's flowers could only be found in moonlight. As a fern, however, it has no flowers, so anyone searching for them would have a fruitless night.

MOSCHATEL
(Adoxa moschatelina)

SCOTS: Wee doon clock / Wee toon clock

GAELIC: *Mosgadal*

This little herbaceous plant of ancient woodlands is beautifully named in Scots – the five flowers on each head are arranged like the faces of a town clock on a tower – albeit with one clock face pointing up towards the sun.

MUGWORT
(*Artemisia vulgaris*)

GAELIC: *Cal-diolais* (Caithness); *Groban*; *Ialthus* (South Uist, Eriskay); *Liath-lus* – grey-weed; *Lus an t' seann duine* – old man's plant; *Mór-manta* – big demure plant; *Mughard* – possibly relating to *mugan* = a mug, or *mugart* = a hog

SCOTS: Bowlocks (Shetland); Bulwand (Shetland); Gall wood (Shetland); Grey bulwand (Shetland); Moogard (Caithness); Muggart (Argyllshire, Dumfriesshire); Muggart kail (Morayshire); Mugger / Muggert; Muggins / Muggons (Aberdeenshire, Ulster)

Mugwort is a distinctive robust herb used medicinally, but more commonly as a flavouring in traditional 'gruit' beers – hence the common names, most of which are derived from earlier Anglo-Saxon *mucgwyrt*, so perhaps gives a closer link to the more ancestral Scots names. The Gaelic *mugart* is most likely adopted from neighbouring Scots.

MULLEIN, GREAT AND OTHERS
(*Verbascum thapsus*)

ENGLISH: Aaron's rod; Adam's flannel; Blanket leaf; Cow's lungwort; Hag's taper; Hog's taper; Shepherd's club

GAELIC: *Bo-choinneal* – cow's candle; *Coinneal Moire* Mary's candle, or sometimes Mary's asthma plant; *Cuineal Mhuire*; *Cuingeal Mhoire* / *Cuingeal Mhuire* – from *cuing* = a narrowing stem, or less likely *cuingeal* = a restraint or shackle; *Lus mór* – big plant; *Lus-na-meala-mór* – great honey plant

SCOTS: Cuddy lugs – donkey's or nag's ears; Schiphird's club; Shepher's club

This chunky, silky-silvery herb with its tall, tapering spikes of yellow flowers is so very striking it's no surprise it picked up a host of names. Used widely as a medicine in respiratory complaints of humans and cattle, it was also a reasonable impromptu switch for driving sheep without harming them.

MUSHROOM, FIELD

(*Agaricus campestris* and *Agaricus bisporus*)

GAELIC: *Balg bhuachaill* – shepherd's bag; *Balg bhuachair* – dung bag; *Balg losgainn* – frog's bag; *Balgan-beice* – little bag of courtesseay; *Balgan-beiceach* – although usually for puffballs; *Balgan-beucan*; *Beacan* – an archaic name, possibly 'bee smotherer'; *Bocan-bioras* – pointed sprite from *Bocan* = hobgoblin/ sprite and *bioras* = sharp/pointed; *Bochdan-beucach*; *Boinead-smachain*; *Boineid smagain*; *Boineid-smachain*; *Bonaid bhuidhli smachain*; *Bonaid smachan*; *Caileag an achaidh*; *Caochag* – nut without a kernel/empty shell; *Fas-air-an-oidhche*; *Leirin-sugach* – possibly pleasant sight from *leir* = sight and *sugach* = pleasant; *Meall-connain*; *Sgeallag a bhuachair / Sgàileag a' bhuachair* – from *sgeallag* = wild mustard and *buachar* = dung

SCOTS: Mushrumps; Paddeh-stuill / Puddock stool

Mushrooms and other fungi have seemingly had a sinister reputation in Scotland, such that they were seldom eaten. The field mushroom and a few species such as chanterelles (*Cantharellus cibarius*) were probably collected and eaten more than others until Victorian times, when collecting widened out, however there has never been a tradition comparable to that on the continent. Many of the names here apply to a wide range of mushrooms, such as the distantly related puffballs (*Lycoperdon* species).

The wonderful little bird's nest
fungi are several species of *cyathus*,
crucibulum and *nidularium*. They
form a nest-like cup containing small,
dispersible egg-like structures called
'peridioles'. These weird mushrooms
were known in Scots as 'siller cups' –
like a cup with silver coins in it.

N

NAVELWORT
(*Umbilicus rupestris*)

ENGLISH: Jack-in-the-bush; Kidney-wort; Lover's links; Maid-in-the-mist

GAELIC: *Còrnan caisil* – a cup or drinking horn; *Lamhan cat leacain / Lamhainn cat leacainn* – hill-cat, or wildcat's gloves; *Lamhan cat leacainn*; *Leacan* – from *leacann* = the broad side of a hill; *Loan cat*

SCOTS: Walpenny woort

A succulent little plant of walls and shady, moist cliffs, the taxonomic and English common name comes from the round, dimpled leaves reminiscent of a bellybutton. The flower spikes bear small, bell-like greenish flowers, which could be seen as looking like gloves – at a stretch.

NETTLE
(*Urtica dioica*)

GAELIC: *Caol-fail* – slender one of the pigsty; *Deanntag* – perhaps from *feannta* 'to flay' because of the sting; *Eanntag*; *Feanndag*; *Feanndagach*; *Feanntag* (Sutherland, Lorne); *Ionntag / Iontag / Iuntag*; *Loiteag* – from *lot* = a wound; *Neandog / Neanntag*; *Stradag* – spark or sting (Hebrides)

SCOTS: Heg beg; Nittle; Stinger

Along with dandelion and daisy, nettle is one of those rare plants that everyone can identify. Although the list of names looks long, many of the Gaelic names feature a few similar-sounding variants and modifications of words for wounding or flaying. However, nettles were certainly not all villainous – they were an important component of tonics and porridges through the springtime, a source of dye and mordant, and a source of fibres, so it is perhaps a bit odd that so few names pick up on these positive aspects, but a sting is more memorable, to be fair.

NIGHTSHADE, DEADLY
(*Atropa belladonna*)

ENGLISH: Dwale; Jacob's ladder / Jaucob's ladder

GAELIC: *An Deagha*; *Lus na oidhche* – night weed/plant of the night

SCOTS: Daft-berries – of the fruits (Forfarshire); Deil's churn staff; Mekilwort / Mekkilwort / Muckle wort – big or great plant

A robust plant with a sinister reputation, deadly nightshade may not be truly native in Scotland, but is widely found throughout warmer coastal regions near towns and cities. It was used medicinally to procure sleep and act as a form of anaesthetic, but the danger of overdose and its possible use to induce hallucinations gave it associations with witchcraft. It is recorded as one of the poisons used to stupefy an invading Danish army. 'Jacob's ladder' is more commonly used for *Polemonium*, a group of plants we normally associate with gardens.

NIGHTSHADE, ENCHANTER'S
(*Circaea lutetiana*)

GAELIC: *Fuinnseach* – playing the wanton as the hooked fruits catch onto clothes, or possibly earth-dryer; *Fuinseagach*; *Lus an talaidh* – enticing, enchanting, luring plant; *Lus na h' oidhnan*; *Lus na h'-oighe* – the maiden's plant

A delicate, slender little plant of shady ancient woodlands, enchanter's nightshade was always seen as magical – the scientific name references both Circe, the enchantress from the Odyssey, and Lutetia – ancient Paris, the hangout of all the best alchemists. Apparently, in Scotland, this plant was secretly fed by girls to boys that they fancied.

NIPPLEWORT
(*Lapsana communis*)

GAELIC: *Duilleag Bhrighde* – Brigid's leaf; *Duilleag-bhràghad / Duilleog-bhràghad / Duilleog-bhraigh* – breast-leaf; *Duilleag-Brighde / Duilleag-Bhrighid / Duilleag-mhaith* – the good leaf; *Duilleag-mhin*; *Son duilleag* – the good leaf

SCOTS: Bolgan – from Bolga, a swelling or bulge

This plant was used in northern Europe as a treatment for mastitis (an infection of the breast tissue).

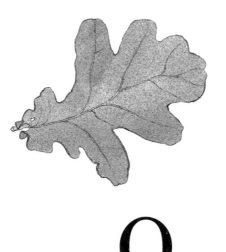

O

OAKS
(*Quercus* species)

GAELIC: *Crann-daraich / Craobh-dharaich* – oak tree; *Dair / Daire*; *Darach / Darag*; *Darire / Darroch / Dharaich*; *Gasagach* – small-stalked pedunculate oak; *Dearc-dharaich*; *Dru*; *Dur*; *Eitheach* – mostly pedunculate oak; *Furran*; *Om / Omna* – mostly pedunculate oak; *Rail*; *Righ na coille* – King of the wood (Highland); *Tuilm* – also for Elm (*Ulmus*)

SCOTS: Aik / Ake / Eak; Knappars / Knapparts / Knappers / Knapperts – of the galls (N Scotland); Moss aik / Moss-oak – oak bogwood; Nut-gall – of the galls; Pipe (SE Scotland); Puggie pipe – the acorn of pedunculate oak on its stalk; Yik (S Scotland)

Oaks loom large in the Scottish consciousness, particularly through their long-standing associations in Celtic myth and legend – whether from classical times or through the misty-eyed revival of the 19th and 20th centuries. *Darroch* appears in many place names throughout Scotland, both ancient and modern. The two native species are slightly different in their habitat preferences and distribution, with the larger pedunculate oak, or English oak (*Quercus robur*) widespread, but a bit more prevalent in the south and west, while the iconic west-coast rainforest oaks of Argyll and the western Highlands are the sessile

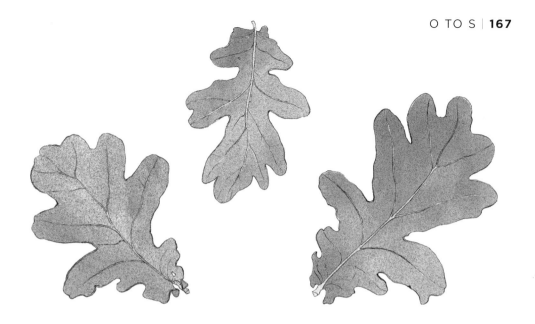

oak (*Quercus petraea*). Both species support an incredible diversity of other organisms. Of these, the many types of galls formed by insects, mites and fungi on the trees are fascinating, and several of the more striking ones have picked up names in Scots. Oak apples, caused by several species of gall wasp, are known as 'nut-galls' in Scots as they seldom reach apple proportions in the shorter Scottish summer, while 'knappers' or 'knapperts' refers to the distorted acorns produced by another gall-wasp, *Andricus quercuscalicis*.

Some of the more iconic species of non-native oaks have also picked up the names *Quercus suber*, while the Mediterranean cork oak is *airc* (cork) or *crann aircann* (cork tree) in Gaelic, although it does not survive this far north. The holm oak (*Quercus ilex*) is another Mediterranean species but grows happily in warmer parts of Scotland. Like the cork oak it is evergreen, so most of its names refer to this. *Crann-tuilm* and *craobh thuilm* are 'knoll' or 'holm-tree', *thuilm*, *tin* and *tolm* mean evergreen, and *darach sior-uaine* is the fully descriptive 'evergreen oak'.

Oak represents the letter D in the Gaelic alphabet of tree names as *Dair*.

OAT
(*Avena sativa*)

GAELIC: *Coirc / Coirce / Corc / Corca*

SCOTS: Ait / Aits / Ait-seed; Awn – often archaic; Corbie aits – black oats, perhaps *Avena strigosa*; Dour seed – archaic; Eat / Eit – from the 16th and 17th centuries; Gray oats; Grits; Hasterns – archaic; Haver / Haver-straw; Oncorn / Uncorn – early 16th century; Ote; Rag – archaic; Redland oats; Rissom; Sandie oat; Shiak / Shiaks; Small oats; Suggeroun – late 16th and early 17th centuries; Tap pickle; Tatie-ait / Tawtie-ait; Yett / Yetten / Yit

As the huge array of names attests, the many different varieties of this fairly hardy grain have long been a staple part of the Scots diet. Many of the names relate to particular varieties suited to different conditions.

OAT-GRASS, FALSE
(*Arrhenatherum elatius*)

ENGLISH: Earthnut; Tall oat grass

GAELIC: *Feur Coirce Brèige* – false oat grass

SCOTS: Arnut; Pight aits; Knot; Swine's arnuts

A robust grass reminiscent of oats, the tuberous base of the plant is quite like that of pignut (*Conopodium majus*), which is also known as arnut (i.e. earth nut, or earth-knot) in Scots.

ORACHE
(*Atriplex patula*)

GAELIC: *Airgeadach Chaol*; *Ceathramha luain griollog*; *Ceathramhan luain griollag* – loin quarters; *Ceathramhan caorach* – sheep's quarters; *Labaid*; *Praiseach mhin* – small meal (*min* = meal, ground fine), or mealy pot.

This coastal and wasteground plant is covered in a waxy protective coating that looks like a thick dusting of flour.

ORCHIDS
(*Dactylorrhiza, Orchis* and other genera)

GAELIC: *Clachan ghadhair* – hound's stones; *Cuigeal-an-losgainn* – frog's spindle; *Lus an talaidh* – the enticing plant; *Moth-ùrach* – earth-male or earthy male. Orchids with spotted leaves are *Dobhrach-bhallach*; *Sobhrach bhallach* and *Urach bhallach* – some of these names reference primroses and other attractive flowering plants as well

SCOTS: Aaron's beard; Adam and Eve; Adder's grass (Berwickshire); Baldeeri / Baldeerie / Balderry/ Boldeeri (Shetland), Beldairy (Aberdeenshire); Bog hyacinth (Kirkcudbrightshire); Bull-bags (Angus); Bull-seg; Cain and Abel (Berwickshire); Cock's came / Cock's Kame – cock's comb; Craw-taes – crow's toes; Crowfoot; Curlie-doddy – curly head; Dead man's fingers (Berwickshire); Dead man's hand (Berwickshire); Deadman's thooms; Deil's foot (Berwickshire); Fool's stones (Orkney); Hens (Berwickshire); Hen's kames – hen's combs (Berwickshire); Paddy's spindles; Puddock's Spindles – toad's legs (Perthshire)

Orchids are so eye-catching and distinctive that they have picked up a wide array of names. The many species and local variants of the two large genera *Dactylorrhiza* and *Orchis* are difficult to distinguish, even for experienced botanists, so we have taken the liberty of lumping them all in together. Names relate to their wet grassland habitat, the chicken's comb-like array of flowers on the pink species, or to the orchids themselves – the tuberous storage organs under the soil that are reminiscent of bloated fingers or testicles. Of course, it is this last similarity that gives the whole group of plants their name, from Greek 'orchis' = testicle. This means there's a slightly scurrilous undertone to some of the names, such as *lus an talaidh*, while others are simply brazen, such as bull-bags. Several other, less familiar orchids have picked up individual names, but these are relatively few. Twayblade (*Neottia ovata*) is 'two-leaved', so *dà-bhileach*, *dà-dhuilleach* or *dà-dhuilleach coittean*. Others, such as the helleborines, have no recorded distinct names in Scots or are fairly direct and modern transliterations or translations to Gaelic – in this case as *eileabor*. Similarly, frog orchid is *mogairlean losgainn*.

ONION
(*Allium cepa*)

GAELIC: *Cutharlan*; *Sgailaid*; *Siobaid*; *Siobann*; *Sronamh*; *Uinnean*

SCOTS: Ingone; Ingoun; Ingan / Ingon / Ingin / Ongone; Sebowe / Sybae / Sybie / Sybo / Syboe / Sybow; Syes; Tails

Most of the Scots and some of the Gaelic names are derived from older European names, attesting to the importance of these plants in cuisine and medicine throughout Europe and beyond – compare *siobaid, sebow* and, for example the Spanish 'cebolla', from Latin *cebolla*, a little onion. The many local variants of 'onion' in Scots are best exemplified in the hungry person's plea to a Forfar baker to: "Gie's a plain bridie, and an ingin ane an aw."

OX-EYE DAISY
(*Leucanthemum vulgare*)

ENGLISH: Dog-daisy; Wild marguerites

GAELIC: *Am Breinean-brothach* – stinking scabby or possibly stinking king; *Dithean-mor* – the big daisy; *Easbadh-brothach* – scabby vanity or idleness; *Easbuigban* – from the name for scrofula; *Easbuig-ban* – fair bishop; *Lus-an-easbuig* – bishop's weed; *Neòinean mór / Neònan mór* – big daisy

SCOTS: Cairt wheel; Gowan; Horse gowan / Horse-gollan / Horse gowlan; Muckle gowan – giant daisy; Muckle kokkeluri (Shetland); White gowan

This robust daisy-like plant may have been lumped in with stinking chamomile (*Athemis cotula*) for some names, although neither smell particularly nice. The Gaelic names relating to bishops hark back to the plant's use in conjunction with the blessings of a high-ranking churchman to treat scrofula – a kind of lymphatic tuberculosis causing swollen, scabby growths on the neck. Scots names tend more to reference its similarity to a large daisy. 'Horse' or 'dog' variant names of plants are often used to refer to cruder, chunkier or less valued versions in this respect.

OYSTERPLANT
(*Mertensia maritima*)

ENGLISH: Sea Gromwell

GAELIC: *Tiodhlac na Mara*

A rare coastal plant, this succulent member of the borage family is said to taste faintly of oysters but should never be eaten from the wild – it's far too rare!

P

PARSLEY
(*Petroselenium crispum*)

GAELIC: *Fionnas-garaidh*;
Muinean Mhuire – Mary's shoot or
sprout; *Pearsal*; *Pearsluibh*; *Peirsill*

SCOTS: Parsly; Persley

A popular flavouring herb, but
one with a sinister reputation and
associations with the Devil in many
parts of Europe – perhaps the
reason it was brought under
Mary's influence in Gaelic.

PEAR
(*Pyrus* species and cultivars)

GAELIC: *Craobh-pheurain-
fiadhain*; *Mal / Mel*; *Peur*

SCOTS: Auchan; Golden nap /
Gowdnap (Selkirkshire); Hinny-
pear (S Scotland); Longavil;
Longueville; Peer; Worry-carle

As with apples, local names for
particular cultivated varieties of
pears exist.

PENNYWORT, MARSH
(*Hydrocotyle vulgaris*)

GAELIC: *Lus na Peighinn* –
penny plant; *Oibheall uisge* –
(Colonsay)

SCOTS: Sheep rot; Shilling-rot
(Ayrshire); Shilling-grass

An interesting little member of the
carrot family with round leaves
that give it its penny and shilling-
related names, while the 'rot'
element is common in many plants
of marshy habitats as they were
associated with foot-rot in sheep
and other livestock grazing in the
area. The plants were sometimes
thought to cause the disease.

PERIWINKLE
(*Vinca species*)

GAELIC: *Faoch*; *Faochag*
Faochag-na-gille-fuinbrin –
little periwinkle of the white lad;
Faochag-na-gille-fuinnbrinn;
Gilleacha-fionn; *Gilleacha-fionn-*
truim; *Gille-fiondrain*; *Gille-fionn*;
Gille-fionn-brinn; *Gille-fionn-truim*;
Gille-fiunnd

Most of these names come from
a fairly close translation of
'periwinkle', the spiral-shelled
mollusc popular as a food. Not
native as far north as Scotland,
this plant is widely introduced in
shady gardens and often escapes.
The lilac-blue flowers of this
creeping evergreen plant are the
definitive periwinkle blue.

PIGNUT

(*Conopodium majus*)

ENGLISH: Earthnut; Lousy earth-nuts

GAELIC: *Braoan* – fairy hill bulb; *Braonan* / *Praonan* – bud of the briar; *Braonan bachlaig* – bud of the shoot; *Braonan bhuachail* / *Braonan-bachuill* / *Braonan-bhuachaille* – shepherd's bud, nut or drop; *Braonan coille* – bud of the wood; *Caor thalmhainn* – nut of the ploughed land/nut of the earth; *Cnò-thalmhainn* – earth nut; *Coirean-muice* – pig nut; *Cutharlan* – a plant with bulbous roots

SCOTS: Arnit / Arnut / Arnuts; Cronies; Curlund / Curluns; Gourlins (Kirkcudbrightshire); Gowlins (Inverness-shire); Horneck / Hornecks (SW Scotland); Knot-girse; Knotty meal (Inverness-shire, Morayshire); Lizzie arnut / Lousey arnut / Lousey earnit; Lousy arnuts; Lousy earnit; Yarnuts

Pignut is one of those classic forageable foods – the dense, nutty flesh of its root tubers are a suitable reward for what is often a tough dig. Children and adults alike ate them regularly – and some still do if they feel confident of identifying them. It's easy to see how such a beloved snack could have garnered so many names. 'Knotty meal' is interesting as it does describe the rough surface of the tuber but is reminiscent of the Gaelic *cairmeal* –applied to the similar tuber of bitter vetch or heath pea (*Lathyrus linifolius*).

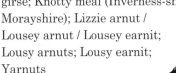

PLANTAIN, GREATER
(*Plantago major*)

ENGLISH: Rat-tail plantain; Way bread; Wayfaring leaf

GAELIC: *Cruach-Phadruig –* Patrick's hill; *Cuach-Phadruig –* Patrick's bowl; *Slan-lus –* healing plant

SCOTS: Bird's meat (Aberdeenshire); Healin' blade / Healin leaf (Caithness, Shetland); Johnsmas flowers; Johnsmas pairs; Lady's nit/ Leddy's nit; Rat tail / Rat's tails; Ripple-girs / Ripple-girse; Tirlie-tod; Wabran / Wabran leaf; Wabret (Borders); Warba (Caithness); Waverin leaf / Wavverin leaf (Orkney and Shetland); Wayburn leaf (Lanarkshire)

A distinctive plant of grasslands, this species is native to western Eurasia, but has become notorious as a weed in countries where it has been introduced – perhaps most famously in North America, where it has come to be known as 'white man's footsteps', as its trample-resistant habit means it is particularly common by pathways. This propensity for wayfaring has been adopted into some of the Scots names, while others, as well as the Gaelic names, reference its importance as a healing leaf – used to treat grazes and burns. In part this value as a medicine is responsible for it being carried around the globe.

PLANTAIN, RIBWORT
(*Plantago lanceolata*)

ENGLISH: Soldiers

GAELIC: *Bodach dhubh*;
Bodach dubh; *Bodaich dhubha* –
the black old man or men; *Deideag* –
row of young teeth or plaything;
Ilus; *Lus an t'slanuchaidh* /
Lus na slan – healing plant;
Lus nan saighdearan; *Lus-an-t-
Slanachaidh*; *Slalus*; *Slàn-lus* –
healing plant; *Slisneach*; *Snaithlus*;
Snathlus (South Uist, Eriskay)

SCOTS: Carl doddies /
Carl-doddie / Carl-doddy /
Carl-dodie; Curl-doddy / Curl-dodie
(E Scotland and Lanarkshire);
Fechters – fighters; Hard-heid /
Hard-heids; Headmanv (Shetland);
Johnsmas flooer; Kemp – *kemp* =
to fight (Selkirkshire); Kempseed;
Ribgrass (Kirkcudbrightshire,
Wigtownshire); Ripple-grass;
Sodger / Sodgers; Warba blades
(NE Scotland)

This common trailside plant and
lawn-weed was, and is, used in a
similar way to its broader-leaved
relative as a treatment for scrapes
and burns, hence many of the
Gaelic names relating to healing.
In contrast, the Scots names
emphasise their use in the battle
game a bit like conkers, where
you and your opponent each take
a flower stalk and take turns
trying to whip the head off your
rival's fechter.

POLYPODY
(*Polypodium* species)

GAELIC: *Ceis chrainn* – basket or tax of the tree; *Clach-raineach* – stone fern; *Clach-raineach chaol*; *Cloch-reathneach Mearlag* / *Meurlag* – probably from *meur* = finger, which the pinnules resemble (Lochaber); *Raineach nan crag* / *Raineach nan creag* – rock fern; *Reidh-raineach* – smooth fern; *Sgeamh* – beauty; *Sgeamh nan clach* / *Sgeamh nan cloch* – beauty or ornament of the rocks

SCOTS: Creyt; Ernfern / Hernfern

Polypodies are small ferns often found on rocks and crags or as epiphytes on trees. Jamieson (1808) suggests the Scots 'Ern fern' – 'eagle fern' may relate to its habitat on these haunts of eagles:

'Found on high rocks. It might hence seem to have received its designation, these being the abode of the eagle or *ern*'

However, the name is also used for bracken (*Pteridium aquilinum*) and similar chunky, ground-dwelling ferns reminiscent of an eagle in flight.

PONDWEEDS
(*Potamogeton* species)

GAELIC: *Duileasg na h'aibhne* – river leaf / river dulse; *Duille-bhaite* (Colonsay); *Linne-lus* – pondweed/pond plant, from *linne* = a pond or poll; *Liobhag* – smooth, polished from the texture of the leaves; *Rafagach* (South Uist, Eriskay); *Seileachan Coitcheann*; *An seileachan, An* – the little willow

SCOTS: Deil's spoons

A group of diverse and difficult to identify plants of still or flowing waters. Names are generally applied equally to the larger-leaved species without distinguishing one scientific species from another.

POPPY
(*Papaver rhoeas* and *P. dubium*)

ENGLISH: Red poppy and field poppy are *Papaver rhoeas*

SCOTS: Blavers, Cockeno, Cockrose, Collinhood; Puppie (mostly for *Papaver rhoeas*)

GAELIC: *Beilbheag / Meilbheag* – little pestle, which the capsule resembles; *Blath-nam-bodach* – old men's flower; *Cathlach-dearg* – Catholic red; *Crom-lus / Cromlus* – bent weed; *Fothros* – corn rose; *Iothros* – from *ioth* = corn and *ros* = rose; *Paipean ruadh* – red/reddish poppy; *Paipin* – from *Papaver* = poppy; *Purpaidh* – purple

The two most familiar species are the red-petalled common poppy (*Papaver rhoeas*) and paler orange long-headed poppy (*P. dubium*), and both are largely interchangeable in naming. The opium poppy (*Papaver sominiferum*) is *codalan* in Gaelic – the procurer of sleep, a name also applied to mandrake (*Mandragora officinarum*).

POTATO
(*Solanum tuberosum*)

GAELIC: *Barra-gug* / *Barr-guc* / *Barr-guchd* / *Barr-gug*; *Buntàta* / *Bun-tàta*; *Slis* (South Uist, Eriskay)

SCOTS: Bloom(s) / Blume(s) – flowers or tops of the plants; Brock; Chun; Pitato; Pitawtie; Ploom / Ploume / Plum – the fruit of the plant; Red nib / Reid nib / Ris nib – an archaic name for a red-skinned variety; Tatie; Tatie bloom – flower or tops of the plant; Tatie ploom – fruit of the plant; Tattie / Tawtie; Tattie / Tawtie bloom – flower or tops of the plants; Tattie / Tawtie ploom – fruit of the plant; Tattie / Tawtie shaw – tops of the plants; Yam

The plant of the mighty chip – 'tattie' is perhaps the most ubiquitous Scots word in modern use today.

PRIMROSE
(*Primula vulgaris*)

GAELIC: *Loisdean*; *Lus-nam-mùisean* / *Mùisean* – a dodgy character or the Devil; *Samhaircean* – pleasure / delight or joy; *Sobhrach* / *Sobhrachan*/*Sobhrag*; *Sobrach* / *Sobrag* / *Soirigh* – pleasure/delight or joy

SCOTS: Buckie-faalie / Buckie-faulie; May flooer; May spink / Mey-spink; Maysie / Meysie; Pimrose; Pink; Plumrocks; Plumrose; Spink

The cheerful yellow primrose is widely known and welcomed in high spring, so the reference to the Devil in *mùisean* is a little unclear. This name is also used for the related cowslip (*Primula veris*).

PUFFBALLS

(*Lycoperdon* species. *Calvatia gigantea* is the giant puffball)

ENGLISH: Blind-man's ball; Fuzz-ball; Devil's snuffbox

GAELIC: *Balg dubh* – black bag; *Balg seididh / Balgan-seididh* – (little) bellows; *Balg-smuid* – smoke bag; *Balgan-beice / Balgan-beiceach*; *Balgan-beucan*; *Balg-peitach / Balgan-peitach* – perhaps from *peitach* = wearing a jacket, so a bag wearing a jacket, although *Balag peitach bocan* is interpreted as the goblin's bag; *Beac / Beacan* – bee (smotherer); *Bocan-bearrach*; *Bocan-biorach*; *Bochdan-bearrach*; *Bochdan-biorrach*; *Boineid-an-losgainn* – toad's bonnet from *boineid* = bonnet and *losgann* = frog/toad; *Caochag* – nut without a kernel/empty shell; *Pocan-beucach* – poor person's bag; *Trioman / Troman*

SCOTS: Blinmen's baw; Buff; Deid man's sneechin – of the spore cloud's similarity to snuff; Fiesti-baa; Fuz-baw / Fuzbaw; Guffa-buggie – puff-bag

Many of the names pick up on the form of these distinctive fungi as effectively a bag full of spore-bearing hyphal structures. These are often dark in many species, hence *balg-dubh* is applied even to the shining white giant puffball. The delightfully flatulent appearance of the spores puffing up is drawn out in the taxonomic name *Lycoperdon* (from Greek 'wolf's fart'), but the names in Scotland are a bit more staid and proper. References to smoke probably allude to the puff of spores, although they were flattened and burned by beekeepers to produce smoke to make bees drowsy – hence the Gaelic *beac* and *beacan*.

QUAKING-GRASS
(*Briza* species – especially *Briza media*)

ENGLISH: Mountain flax (Kirkcudbrightshire), Silver shackles

GAELIC: *Ceann-air-chrith* – quaking grass; *Coirce-circe* – hen's oats; *Conan / Conan cumanta* – hound or hero, common hare or rabbit; *Crith-fheur* – quaking grass; *Feur gort / Feur gortach* – starving grass; *Feur-sithean sithe* – fairy or phantom breath of wind; *Grigleann* – cluster or festoon (Breadalbane)

SCOTS: Shak-an-tremble; Shaker(s), Shakie, Shakie tremlies, Siller shackles (Borders); Siller shaker (Borders); Tremlies

The plump silvery heads of this delicate little grass shiver and rustle in the breeze, giving rise to many of its names.

R

RADISH
(*Raphanus raphanistrum* and *R. maritimus*)

ENGLISH: Sea radish (*Raphanus maritimus*)

GAELIC: *Curran-dearg* – red carrot; *Meacan ruadh* – reddish plant; *Meacan-dearg*; *Meacan-ruadh*; *Racadal*; *Raibhe*; *Raidis*

SCOTS: Charlock; Gool; Guilde; Runch / Runchie / Runchik; Ryfarts

Most of these names relate to the garden radish rather than the wild ancestral type.

RAGGED ROBIN
(*Silene flos-cuculi*)

GAELIC: *Brog na feannaige* – crow's shoes (South Uist, Eriskay); *Caorag lèana* – marsh spark; *Cirein coilich* (Barra); *Currac-cubhaige* – Cuckoo's cap; *Flur-na-cubhaig* / *Plur-na-cubhaig* – Cuckoo flower; *Lus siode* – silk-weed

SCOTS: Cock's caim; Meadow spink; Rag-a-tag (Shetland)

The deeply cleft silky petals of this marsh-dwelling member of the carnation family are unmistakeable. *Caorag lèana* – the marsh spark is among the most apt names for any plant – as the flowers look like little fireworks in the green. Like the other Cuckoo flower (*Cardamine pratensis*), it begins to blossom in late April and early May – around the time cuckoos return, although both may still be found blooming into August.

RAGWORT
(*Senecio jacobea*)

ENGLISH: Ragweed; Witch's horses

GAELIC: *As na gineamh* (South Uist, Eriskay); *Ballan buidhe* (Colonsay); *Ballan-boidhe* / *Ballan-buidhe* – yellow tub; *Buadharlann* – the stripling or branch that overcomes i.e. takes over; *Buadhghan buidhe* / *Buaghallan bhuidhe*; *Buailtean* (Gairloch); *Cuiseag* / *Guiseag* – a stalk; *Cuiseag bhuidhe* / *Guiseag bhuidhe* – yellow-stalk; *Geostan*

SCOTS: Beaweed; Benweed; Bowlocks (Wigtownshire); Bundweed / Bunwede – from *bun* / *bon* = begging, so beggar's weed; Curly doddie / Curly doddies; Ell-shinders (Aberdeenshire, Ayrshire, Berwickshire, Lothian); Elstinders; Fizz-gig (Aberdeenshire, Ayrshire, Berwickshire, Lothian); Gollan / Golland; Ragweed (Berwickshire, Lothian, Ayrshire, Aberdeenshire); Sinking Alisander / Stinking Alisander (Stirlingshire); Sleepy-dose; (Banffshire); Stinking Davie / Stink-Davie; Stinking weed; Stinking Willie; Wee bo / weebo – a little devil; Weebie; Yellow weed (Berwickshire)

This important agricultural weed is a source of yellow dye and was used for basketry in Shetland, but typically had a bad reputation as it is toxic to livestock. Hence, we see several devilish names and references to 'stink'. The plant does not smell *too* offensive, however, so it is more its reputation as a weed that makes it stink. The Scots names alluding to Doddie (George) or Willie (William) may well be sectarian in origin, although the Alexander and Alisander may come from the similarities to the invasive yellow-flowered umbellifer known as Alexanders (*Smyrnium olusatrum*). The reference to witch's horses is picked up in several pieces of poetry and literature through the 16th to 18th centuries, again, reflecting the low regard in which the plant was held.

RASPBERRY
(*Rubus idaeus*)

ENGLISH: Rasp / Wood rasp (Selkirkshire)

GAELIC: *Brigh nan craobh*; *Preas subh chraobh*; *Preas-shuidheag*; *Sivven*; *Sùbh / Sùbhag / Sùbh-craoibh / Sughag / Suibheag / Suibhean* – sappy bush; *Suth-craobh* (Colonsay)

SCOTS: Himberry; Hindberry – as eaten by deer; Siven / Sivven; Thummles – thimbles, describing the fruit

A probable wild native plant long since domesticated, the raspberry is one of the staples of gardens and a core part of the berry industry of the Mearns and Tay valley.

REDCURRANT
(*Ribes rubrum*)

ENGLISH: Wineberry

GAELIC: *Dearc-dhearg*; *Dearcan dearga*; *Dearc-an-Fhrangach* – probably French berry; *Raosar dearg*; *Spriunan*

SCOTS: Raser / Rissert / Rizar / Rizzar; Rizzles; Russer berre; Russle / Russles

Red and blackcurrants (*Ribes nigrum*) grow well in Scotland, although *dearc an Fhrangah* (French berry) suggests their introduction to cuisine around the late mediaeval period in Gaelic-speaking areas. Most of the Scots names are tied to the red of the berries.

REDSHANK
(*Persicaria maculosa*)

ENGLISH: Spotted knotweed;
Useless

GAELIC: *Boinne-fola, am* –
the blood spot; *Glùineach dhearg*;
Glùineach mhor – the big-kneed
or jointed plant; *Gluinteach*
(South Uist, Eriskay); *Lus chrann
ceusaidg / Lus chrann ceusaidh* –
herb of the crucifixion tree

SCOTS: Dead arsemart /
Dead arsmart / Spotted arssmart;
Flooering soorick (Shetland);
Yellowin' girse (Shetland)

This plant's swollen nodes (joints)
and the reddish-purple spot on the
leaves give it many of its names.

REED
(*Phragmites australis* and others)

ENGLISH: Loch reed; Star reed

GAELIC: *Biorah lachanm /
Biorcah lachanm / Biorrach lachan*;
Crann-cuilce / Cuilc / Cuile – cane,
perhaps from Latin *culmus* = stalk
or Greek 'kalamos' = reed; *Feadan* –
reed; *Lachan*; *Reudan*; *Ribheid*;
Seasg / Seasgan / Seisg / Seisgeann –
reed/reeds

SCOTS: Sprat / Sprot; Stower;
Streed

Many of these names may overlap
with other reedy waterside species,
so *seisg* is a general term that
roughly equates to 'reed' rather
than any one species. However,
lachan is considered more specific.

RESTHARROW
(*Ononis* species)

ENGLISH: Purple restharrow without prickles (*O. repens*); Spiny restharrow (*O. spinosa*)

GAELIC: *Sreang bogha / Sreang thrian / Trian tarraing / Trian tarrainn* – bow-string; *Sreang Bogha Bhiorach* (*O. spinosa*)

SCOTS: Cammock / Cummock – perhaps related to 'bow-string' from *cam* = crooked, like a pulled bow-string; Lady-whin (Morayshire); Sitfast / Sitfasts (Morayshire); Wild liquorice (Dumfriesshire, Inverness-shire, Morayshire)

The tough, running rhizomes of restharrow are very difficult to plough through, which most of these names reflect – like trying to cut through a bow-string. Lady-whin references the similarity of this species to whin or gorse (*Ulex europaeus*). Both are members of the pea family from similar habitats. Restharrow is much smaller and with pink, rather than yellow, petals.

ROCK-SAMPHIRE
(*Crithmum maritimum*)

GAELIC: *Cnàmh-lus / Lus nan cnamh* – chewing or digestive weed; *Gairgean-creagach* – rock garlic; *Grillog* – loin; *Saimbhir*

SCOTS: Pasper / Paspier / Passper (SW Scotland)

This cliff-dwelling member of the carrot family was collected and eaten as a digestive aid. The '-phire', '-*bhir*' and '-per' elements of the names are thought to reference St. Peter, drawing in the pun of Greek 'petra' – rock.

ROCKROSE
(*Helianthemum nummularium*)

GAELIC: *Flur na greine* / *Plur na greine* – sunflower; *Grian ros* / *Grian-ròs* – sun rose; *Feur Rèisg Ghoirt*

SCOTS: Solflower

A cheerful flower of sandy and rocky, well-drained spots from coast to mountains. The name *Feur Rèisg Ghoirt* is a difficult one to interpret, potentially translating to 'saltmarsh grass' which does not really describe this plant in any way, so may indicate a misrecording of the name.

ROSEROOT
(*Sedum rosea*)

ENGLISH: Priest's pintel (Banffshire); Sea dollies (Banffshire)

GAELIC: *Crasag* – bloated; *Lus nan laoch* – hero's plant; *Lus nan laogh* – calf's plant; *Maraiche* – sailor

A beautiful tufted succulent plant of cliffs and rocky spots from sea level to the heights of Ben Lawers. The English name is simple and accurate – the root (and rhizome) smell of roses. As a consequence, the plant was used as a deodorant for clothing, but also as a purgative for calves during springtime. *Maraiche* is a common name for coastal plants.

ROSES
(*Rosa* species)

ENGLISH: Burnet rose (*Rosa spinosissima*)

GAELIC: *Dreas nam Mucag* – (Colonsay); *Ròs Beag Bàn na h-Alba* – little white rose of Scotland

SCOTS: Cat-hep – cat's hip, the fruit of the species (Berwickshire)

The lovely, white-flowered coastal species is very different from most other species in Scotland, so is pulled out as distinct, and is the usual one recognised as the Jacobean Scottish rose.

ROSE, DOG
(*Rosa canina*)

GAELIC: *Coin droighionn* – dog's thorn; *Coin ròs* / *Ròs nan Con* – dog's rose; *Earradhris* – armed with thorns; *Faileag* – a jewel; *Feardhris* – armour; *Fearra-dhris* – a jewel; *Preas-mhucag* / *Preas-nam-mucag* – little pig's bush; *Sgeach-mhadraidh* – dog's haw; *Boghmuc* / *Bo-muc* (South Uist, Eriskay)

SCOTS: Choops; Dog-hipp; Dog-tippens; Hepthorn – hip thorn; Itchy coo (central and E Scotland); Klonger / Klunger (Shetland); Muckack / Muckie (Caithness, Ross-shire and Inverness-shire)

Many of the names listed under dog rose (*Rosa canina*) are probably applicable to a wide range of other species and hybrids as they are a diverse and difficult group to identify. 'Itchy coos' are notorious as the achenes, the little fruits inside the hip, which are covered in stiff irritant hairs – many can remember the itch of having them dropped down our backs – ah the joys of schooldays!

ROWAN
(Sorbus aucuparia)

ENGLISH: Mountain ash

GAELIC: *Caor* – the berry (Colonsay); *Caora-caorthainn*; *Caorann*; *Caorthainn*; *Caorunn* – berry, usually the Rowan; *Chaoruin*; *Coille* – woodland; *Craobh chaoran* / *Craobh-chaorainn* – berry tree; *Fuinnseag-coille* – the wood enchantress; *Luis* – a drink; *Luisreog* – a charm; *Uinseag*

SCOTS: Quicken; Rantree / Rauntree (Roxburghshire); Raun / Roan / Rone; Roden / Rodden / Roddin (NE Scotland); Roun / Rountree

Roden and similar names, such as rone, ron and runn were more widely applied to other small trees and shrubs, perhaps implying that the Rowan was an exemplar – the definitive small tree. Similarly, *caorunn* can apply more widely to other red berries. As biologist John Lightfoot explains in *Flora Scotica* (1777), people from the Highlands distilled the fruit into a very good spirit and used it as a charm to protect against witchcraft. Indeed – many garden gates have rowans planted beside them in at least a nod to this tradition today – to protect against evil magic.

RUE
(Thalictrum and *Ruta* species)*

GAELIC: *Rù*; *Rù Beag* / *Ru beg* – *Thalictrum*; *Rugh* / *Ruigh*; *Rù*; *Ru gharaidh* – garden rue, *Ruta graveolens*; *Ruadhlus, An* – the rue plant

Although unrelated, the wild (*Thalictrum*) and garden (*Ruta graveolens*) rues look superficially very similar. The latter has a strong pungent smell and was used widely in medicine.

RUSHES
(*Juncus* and other members of the *Juncaceae* family)

GAELIC: *Fead – a* whistle;
Luachair / Luachar

SCOTS: Bennels (S Scotland); Floss;
Rash; Rash bush; Rosh; Sprattie;
Sprottie; Sprotty; Trow bura –
Troll's Rush (Orkney, Shetland)

These terms are used generally for
rushes, with 'sprotty' and related
words also referring to areas covered
in rushes – especially wet pastures
and other grazing land with the
soft rush (*Juncus effusus*) in it.
Although used for making wicks
and impromptu ropes, rushes are
unpalatable to livestock, so often
seen as a bit of an infestation. 'Rash'
and 'rash bush' are probably just
variations on rush but may also hint
at their somewhat invasive nature.

Perhaps the most important
species was *Juncus effusus* –
a tough clump-forming plant of
wet acid grasslands, it is often the
thing left untouched by livestock
in pastures. However, it was an
invaluable thatching material as
it was abundant, and the soft pith
from inside the leaf was coated
in animal fat to make the cheap
but ubiquitous wicks in rush-wick
lamps. This species is particularly
glas-tugha – green thatch or *ur-
luachair* – 'fresh green', and is the
true *luachair bhog*, albeit many
other species share this name.

RUSH, HEATH
(*Juncus squarrosus*)

GAELIC: *Broch-fheur*; *Brù-
chorcachd / Brù-chorcan / Brù-
chorcur*; *Bru-corpan*; *Brùth-chorcan*;
Moran / Muran – name applied to
plants with tapering roots;
Tarraing-air-eiginn – tough to
uproot; *Tarruing-gun-taing*

SCOTS: Burra; Burri-stikkel;
Stuil-bent

This small rush of open moorlands
is seen as being too tough for sheep
or cattle, hence the reference to
grass for the deer. Most of the
names in Scots are from Shetland,
Orkney or the nearby mainland
of Scotland.

RUSH, WOOD
(*Luzula* species – often *Luzula sylvatica*)

GAELIC: *Aithneach*; *Ineach*; *Learman* – clear, obvious; *Luachair Choille* / *Luachair Coille* – bright woodland grass; *Seilisdeir-nan-gobhar* – goat's sunlight or rainbow (Colonsay)

This is a robust, lush plant of woodlands. The bright green leaves are like emerald, especially when dewy, hence several of the names relating to their clarity and luminous nature. They are savoured by rabbits and livestock alike, and their absence in otherwise ancient woodland indicates grazers are around.

RYEGRASS
(*Lolium* species)

ENGLISH: Ray grass; Sturdy grass

GAELIC: *Breòillean*; *Cuiseach* / *Cuiseag* – stalk, straw or weed; *Dìthean* – daisy, perhaps relating to lawns; *Feur-cuir* – grass, perhaps sown-grass; *Feur-seagail* – rye grass; *Roille* – darnel; *Ruintealas*; *Siobhach*

SCOTS: Windlestrae

Ryegrasses are tough grasses of lawns and wild lowland grasslands, including meadows, where they are important forage species. However, darnel (*Lolium temulentum*), which has its own entry in this book, is dangerously toxic, causing hallucinations and tremors. Unfortunately, it is fairly similar to wheat, so was formerly a dangerous weed of agriculture, although much rarer now.

S

SANICLE
(*Sanicula europaea*)

ENGLISH: Wood sanicle

GAELIC: *Bodan coille*; *Bodan couille* – wood tail/little old man of the wood; *Buine* – ulcer; *Raema*; *Reagaim / Reaghim*; *Reagha*; *Reagha maighe*

SCOTS: Sanycle

This strange little member of the carrot family is a classic indicator species for old, species-rich woodland. As the name suggests, it was used in poultices and similar preparations to cleanse ulcers and other sores on the skin.

SCABIOUS, DEVIL'S BIT
(*Succisa pratensis*) and Field (*Knautia arvensis*)

ENGLISH: Devil's bit

GAELIC: *Greim an deabhuill / Greim an diabhail* – devil's bit; *Mhullach*; *Odharach Bhallach* – perhaps ball-topped; *Odharach mhullaich / Odharaich-mhullaich* – yellowish top; *Ura bhallach* – perhaps meaning new ball (*ur* = fresh, *ballach* from ball, or *ballac* = spotted); *Urach mhullaich* – bottle-topped, as *urach* = bottle, *mullach* = top, from shape of the flowerhead

SCOTS: Blue bonnets, Curl doddie / Curl-dodie; Deil's bit

The truncated roots of Devil's bit scabious are said to have been bitten off by the Devil, who was jealous of its virtues and delicate lilac blue flowers. The reference to *odharaich mhullaich* is interesting as it is thought to be a reference to *odhar* (dun or yellow), in spite of the colour of the flowers. It was, however, the source of a yellow dye. Field scabious (*Knautia arvensis*) has larger, pinker flowerheads, but shares many of the same names. However, it is also *bodach gorm* (old blue man) or *gille guirmein* (the blue lad).

SCENTLESS MAYWEED
(*Tripleuropsermum inodorum*) and Sea (*T. maritimum*)

GAELIC: *Buidheag an arbhair* – the corn daisy; *Camomhail fiadhain / Camomhil feadhain* – wild chamomile; *Buidheag na Mara* – sea-daisy is *Tripleurospermum maritimum*

SCOTS: Dog's camovyne; Dog's gowan; Featherwheelie; Feverfoulie; Stinking Tam / Stinking Tammy

These chunky members of the daisy family have typical daisy-like heads (capitula) with yellow central disc florets surrounded by a wheel of white ray florets. These are reminiscent of the true feverfew (*Tanacetum parthenium*), although the scentless and sea mayweeds have far more feathery leaves – hence the superbly descriptive 'featherwheelie', itself a corruption of feverfoulie, another name for feverfew, meaning fever-leaf.

SCOTS LOVAGE
(*Ligusticum scoticum*)

GAELIC: *Luibh an liugair* – cajoler's weed; *Lus nan luagh* – calf's herb; *Shunnis / Siunas / Suinas / Sunais* – a blast of wind or storm

SCOTS: Lovage; Luffage; Scotch parsley; Shemis

This member of the carrot family grows on coastal rocks and was a bit of a Scottish culinary speciality, commonly used as an ingredient in stews, especially with lamb. The flavour is somewhat between parsley and celery.

SCOTS PINE
(*Pinus sylvestris*)

GAELIC: *Cona* – from Greek 'chonos', a cone; *Crann-ghiuthais*; *Craobh-ghiuthais*; *Giubhas / Giudhas / Giuthas / Guibhas* – from *gis* = pitch or resin; *Peith*; *Pin-chrann* – pine tree

SCOTS: Banet fir / Bannet fir / Bonet fir / Bonnet fir / Bunet fir / Bunnet fir (Angus); Burr (Banffshire); Moss fir – bog pine, recovered from peatbogs; Pinule – sapling; Preenack – of the needle; Sheepie – of the cone

Pines generally were referred to as 'firs', as were other large conifers such as spruces, although the 'true' firs are members of the genus *Abies* and spruces are *Picea* species. Scots pine is the only such conifer native to Scotland, with juniper a much smaller shrub, and yew only debatably native. The various 'bonnet' references in Angus specifically mean those large trees where the crown has formed the dense, dark green spreading form reminiscent of a bunnet atop a straight, orange-barked trunk.

***Giuthas* represents the letter G in the Gaelic alphabet of tree names.**

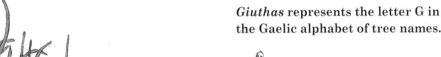

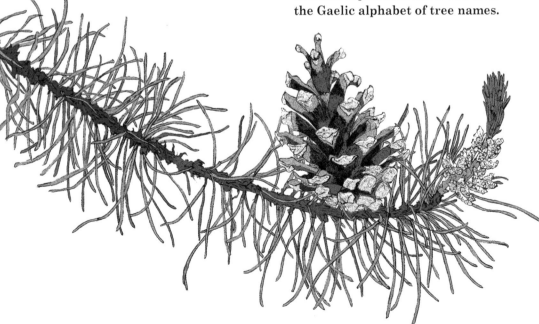

SCURVYGRASS, COMMON
(*Cochlearia officinalis*)

ENGLISH: Spoon-wort

GAELIC: *Amharag / Amharaich* – raw or pungent, of the rocket-like taste; *Carran* – (plant for) scurvy from *carr* = scurvy; *Duine aig am Bheil Carr* – man who has scurvy; *Gille-gig*; *Maraich, Lus an eallain* – island plant; *A / Maraich, A / Mharaich, A* – the sailor; *Plaigh na Carra* – plague of leprosy

SCOTS: Cherlock; Screebie / Screebiegrass / Screeby / Screeviegirse / Scrubie grass

This easily recognised little member of the cabbage family is abundant round most shores and was an important treatment and preventative for scurvy. Tasting like rocket, albeit sometimes dialled up to 11 for flavour, the high content of vitamin C (like many plants), ease of identification and ready coastal availability made it very convenient for sailors. Almost all the names here relate to such elements. The English 'spoon-wort' describes the spoon-like, shiny leaves. *Carran Danmhairceach* is Danish scurvygrass (*Cochlearia danica*), while *Carran Sasannach* is English scurvygrass (*Cochlearia anglica*). In practical terms, little distinction would have been made among these three species.

SEA IVORY
(*Ramalina* species)

ENGLISH: Beard of the Rock, Grey beard lichen

GAELIC: *Feusag ann creag* – beard of the rock; *Fèitheag liath* – grey sinew or vein

These little coastal, rock-dwelling lichens are well-named for their beard-like bristliness.

SEA KALE
(*Crambe maritima*)

GAELIC: *Càl na Mara* – kale of the sea; *Cabaist* – possibly a corruption of cabbage; *Cal* – kale; *Cal colbhairt* – kale with stout fleshy stalks; *Cal-ceirsleach* – curly kale; *Cal-colbhairt* – wild cabbage; *Morran* – wild cabbage; *Praiseach-bhaidhe* – little pot-herb of the wave; *Praiseag tragha* – shore pot-herb; *Rothach tragha* / *Rotheach tragha* – the wheeled one of the shore

This wild relative of domesticated kale and cabbages is an impressive steely blue plant with spherical fruits – perhaps the origin of the reference to 'wheels' in the name *rotheach tragha*.

SEA LETTUCE
(*Ulva lactuca*)

GAELIC: *Glasag* – blue-green; *Slabhagan*; *Slocan*

SCOTS: Lavry

Sea lettuce is unrelated to sloke, or laver (*Porphyra umbilicalis*), although it looks similar, albeit green rather than purplish, and was used in the same way as a food, which is perhaps why they share several names.

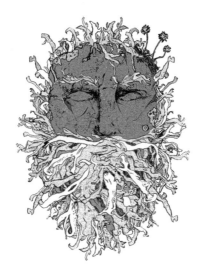

SEA OAK
(*Halidrys siliquosa*)

ENGLISH: Sea fern

GAELIC: *Raineach mhara* – the sea fern

Halidrys means sea oak, but this much-branched brown seaweed looks more like a fern than an oak, so the common names are more sensible than the taxonomic Latin name. The reproductive structures look like the pods of the cabbage family known as siliqua, hence the specific epithet.

SEA ROCKET
(*Cakile maritima*)

ENGLISH: Rocket; Sea gilly-flower

GAELIC: *Gearr bochdan* / *Gearr-bhochdan* – little sprite; *Fearsaideag* – possibly from Irish Gaelic *Saide* = a seat

This coastal member of the cabbage family is slightly succulent and tastes like rocket. The pink flower is similar to that of stocks (*Matthiola* species) or other 'gilly-flowers'.

SEDGES
(*Carex* species)

GAELIC: *Gainnisg / Gainneasag* – sedgey; *Gall-sheilistear* – rainbow or sunlight branch; *Seasg* – barren/unfruitful; *Seilisdeir* – rainbow or sunlight

Several of the Gaelic names for sedges are used in a similar sense to English, to describe the habitat sedges are found in. Although there are dozens of species from all kinds of habitats in Scotland, the larger sedges are often found on wet, and hence unproductive ground, so a 'sedge' is both the plant and the type of spot it is found in.

SELFHEAL
(*Prunella vulgaris*)

ENGLISH: All-heal; Churnwort; Heart o' the Earth; Prince's feather

GAELIC: *Ceanabhan beag* (Colonsay); *Ceann-a-sgadain-dheirg* (Colonsay); *Dubhan ceann chosach* – dark spongy-head, implying an absorptive healing plant; *Dubhanuith*; *An Fèarnach* – like alder (*Alnus glutinosa*); *Lus a chridh / Lus-a'-chridhe* – heart plant; *Slan-lus* – the healing plant; *Tom moighe*; *Tom muighe* (South Uist, Eriskay)

SCOTS: Crochle girs; Hert of the yearth; Puir man's clover

Selfheal, as the common English name implies, was used in healing. Like many other healing plants with dense heads, this compact member of the mint family could be employed 'in the field', with the flowerheads pressed against a wound, although it was widely used throughout Europe in more processed forms for a range of conditions. The Gaelic *an fèarnach* is a bit of a mystery, as the plant and its leaves are unlike alder and it is not particularly from the same habitat or used in the same way. Author Alexander Carmichael mentions *slisneach* as a plant somewhat like *slan-lus*, although its true identity remains a mystery.

SHEEP'S SORREL
(*Rumex acetosella*)

GAELIC: *Fluran-seangan / Pluran-seangain / Pluirean meangan* – small slender flower; *Geoirean / Geoiren*; *Ruanaidh* – reddish coloured; *Samhadh-caora* – sheep's capsule; *Sealbhag nan Caorach* – sheep's sorrel; *Sealbhag chlusach*

These names are fairly specific to sheep's sorrel – although this species probably uses some of the names listed under common sorrel (*Rumex acetosa*) as well.

SHEPHERD'S PURSE
(*Capsella bursa-pastoris*)

ENGLISH: Mother's heart; Lady's garters; Lady's purse (Caithness, Wigtownshire, Ulster); Lady's purses (Berwickshire)

GAELIC: *Luibh-a-sporain* (Colonsay); *Lus na fala / Lus na fola* – blood herb/weed (Colonsay); *Sporan / Sporan buachaille* – the purse, or shepherd's purse; *Sraidean*

SCOTS: Lady's gartens; Leddy's garters; Leddy's purse; Rofle the lady's purses

SILVERWEED
(*Argentina anserina*)

ENGLISH: Dog tansy / Dog's tansy; Fair-days (Berwickshire); Fair grass (Berwickshire); Goose grass (Berwickshire, Roxburghshire); Moor-grass; Swine's beads; Swine's grass (Orkney); Wild skirret

GAELIC: *Bar a bhrigean* / *Bar bhrisgein* – brittle bread, *bar* is an obsolete word for bread; *Briosgean-nan-caorach*; *Briosglan*; *Brisgean* / *Brisghean* (Colonsay, Skye and elsewhere) / *Brisliean* – brittle; *Cerrucan*; *Curran earraich* / *Curran-earrach* – spring carrot; *Seachdamh aran, An* – the seventh bread (Colonsay)

SCOTS: Fair girse; Mascorn / Mascorns; Moss-crop / Moss-crops; Moss-grass; Swine's murriks – pig's roots

The roots of this wonderful little plant were an important source of carbs – hence the references to carrots, bread and skirret. However, the roots in many individuals are tiny, and it is hard to imagine anyone collecting enough for a satisfying meal, let alone some of the tales told of a small patch sustaining a grown man indefinitely. It grows in sandy soils and by paths and its silvery, feather-like leaves are extremely trample-resistant, making it an ideal plant for a flowering lawn.

Skirret (*Sium siasarum*) is a rarely grown traditional vegetable in the carrot family with slender, starchy roots.

SNAPDRAGON
(*Antirrhinum majus*)

GAELIC: *Sron-an-laoigh*; *Srubh-an-loaigh*

SCOTS: Grannie mutch; Mappie's mous; Mop-mop; Moup / Mowp; Mup-mup

An introduced garden ornamental, the snapdragon is very popular and easily identified, with quite a variety of names. The English common name comes from the draconic-looking flowers that can be made to snap open and shut, by gently squeezing the side of the floral tube – hours of fun.

SNEEZEWORT
(*Achillea ptarmica*)

ENGLISH: Hardhead (Ayrshire)

SCOTS: Hard heid / Hard-heids; Moleery tea (Caithness); Pepper girse; Sholgirse; Stolgirse

GAELIC: *Cruaidh-lus* – hard weed; *Lus-a'-chorrain* – herb of the scythe; *Meacan ragaim* / *Meacan roibe* – stiff plant; *Ragaim*; *Roibhe* – moppy, mop-like

Sneezewort is a close relative of yarrow (*Achillea millefolium*), but with far less elaborate leaves. The flowerheads persist as dense little spheres when in fruit, giving them the name hardheads, one that is shared with knapweed (*Centaurea nigra*).

SORREL
(*Rumex acetosa*)

ENGLISH: Sour dock

GAELIC: *Copag shraide* / *Copog shraide* – roadside or lane dock; *Geoirean* – the more bitter or sharper one; *Puinneag* – perhaps from *puinneanach a pugilist* as it was used to heal bruises; *Sabh* / *Samh* / *Sobh* – sorrel; *Sealbhag* – perhaps from *searbh* (sour or bitter) rather than *sealbh* meaning possession; *Sealbhag ruanaidh*; *Sealgag*

SCOTS: Lamb sourocks; Lammie sourocks (Roxburghshire); Rantie-tantie; Redshank (Roxburghshire); Red shank / Reid shank; Sookie soorocks; Soor dock / Soor docken; Soor leek; Sooracks / Soorick / Soorik / Soorocks (Shetland); Soordock; Soukie soorocks; Sour leek; Souries (Aberdeenshire); Sourlick (Roxburghshire); Sourock

A widespread and widely used refreshing leaf with a sour taste, it's no surprise the flavour pops up in so many of these names – the Gaelic shift from *searbh* (sour or bitter) to *sealbh* (possession, property, luck or fortune) is an interesting example of how changes in spelling could readily be picked up and the meaning interpreted differently – although anyone who has tasted lip-smackingly fresh sorrel is fortunate indeed. Sheep's sorrel (*Rumex acetosella*) is a smaller species of rockier habitats, but common enough – this is often called 'lammie sourocks' and variants. Please see the entry for sheep's sorrel for some more names that are specific to that plant. The much rarer mountain sorrel (*Oxyria digyna*) is *sealbhag nam fiadh* – deer's sorrel.

SOUTHERNWOOD
(*Artemisia abrotanum*)

ENGLISH: Lady's love; Old man

GAELIC: *Calltuinn* / *Caltainn* – perhaps from a harbour, or 'to hide'; *Lus an t' seanne duine* – old man's plant; *Meath chaltuinn*; *Meath-chaltainn*

SCOTS: Aipelringie / Aippelringie (NE Scotland); Auld man; Overeengie; Pleuch man's love – ploughman's love; Sidderwuid / Sitherwood / Suddernwood / Suddren wud

Southernwood is not native to Scotland but was introduced centuries ago as a medicinal plant and a flavouring for beers and liquors. The Gaelic *meath* can be interpreted as 'to faint, or be weak,' as the plant was believed to be a tonic against weariness.

SPEARWORTS
(*Ranunculus flammula* and *Ranunculus lingua*)

ENGLISH: Butterplate; Goosetongue; Snake's tongue (Berwickshire)

GAELIC: *Buidheag* – yellow; *Glaisleum* / *Glaisleun* / *Glas-leun* – green-swamp; *Lasair-leana* / *Lesair-leana* – swamp-flame

SCOTS: Wil fire / Wilfire

These upright, slender-leaved buttercups are found in swamps and margins of ponds or canals. The lesser spearwort (*R. flammula*) is more widespread throughout the country, while greater spearwort is most common in the central belt and eastern lowlands. The large, striking flowers of this latter plant perfectly suit the name, 'butterplate'.

SPEEDWELLS
(*Veronica* species)

GAELIC: *Darg thalmhainn*;
Nuallach – howling, lowing or
wailing; *An-Uallach* is Germander
speedwell (*Veronica chamaedrys*);
Lus-crè – dust-plant; *Lus-crè
Monaidh* – mountain dust-plant;
Seamar chre / Seamrag chre –
dust clover is Thyme-leaved
speedwell (*Veronica serpyllifolia*);
Veronica anagallis-aquatica –
the water speedwell is *Fualachdar,
Fualachter* or other variant
spellings, meaning 'the one that
grows in water'

SCOTS: Jennie's blue e'en –
Jennie's blue-eyes is a general
Victorian name for blue-flowered
Veronica species; Blaver; Cat's een /
Cat's e'en and Fluellen are
names for Germander speedwell
(*Veronica chamaedrys*); Foiret is
Scots for Large field speedwell
(*Veronica persica*)

A number of these names are
probably used across several
species, as they are superficially
very similar, but 'Jenny's blue e'en'
is an excellent description for the
bright blue flowers with their twin
stamens curving up a little like
eyelashes. The robust, common and
easily identified aquatic species
Brooklime (*Veronica beccabunga*)
has many more names, so has a
separate entry.

SPHAGNUM

ENGLISH: Bog moss; Flow-moss; White peat

GAELIC: *Coinneach dearg* – red moss; *Fionnlach* – white moss; *Mointeach Liath* – grey peat or moss

SCOTS: Moss

Sphagnum was an extremely important wound dressing, famously so during the world wars, while the peat it forms was an essential source of fuel, as well as a building material. A huge number of other names could be added to this list if we delved into the world of peat in particular, but even these relatively few names show that the plants, places and peat were intimately linked – 'moss' and 'Flow' are names for the extensive peatbogs dominated by *Sphagnum*, as well as the plants themselves. The Gaelic names tend to reference the colour, which changes seasonally or with different levels of drying, and differs among species, ranging from very pale grey-green through to fiery reds and deep purples.

SPIGNEL
(*Meum athamanticum*)

GAELIC: *Bricein-dubh*; *Bricein / Bricin* (Inverness-shire); *Moiken*; *Muilceann / Muilcionn* – aromatic or smelly head

SCOTS: Badminnie; Badmoney; Baldmoney; Bawdmoney; Bawdringie (Perthshire); Bricin; Highland mickim; Jacquin; Meu; Michen / Micken; Moiken; Sinkel

This fairly small but pleasantly pungent member of the carrot family is not common in Scotland but was prized as a flavouring in drinks and cooking. *Michen* and *micken* are probably derived from the Gaelic.

SPURGES
(*Euphorbia* species)

GAELIC: *Buidhean nan ingean* – sea-spurge (*Euphorbia paralias*); *Cranntachan an deamhain*; *Geur-neimh*; *Lus leighis*; *Lus-nan-leusaidh*; *Lus an leigheasaidh* – petty spurge (*Euphorbia peplus*); *Neòinean-puinnsein*; *Spuirse*; *Spuirse-ghréine*; *Spuirse-mhilis* – honey spurge (may apply to any of the strongly honey-scented species)

SCOTS: Deil's churnstaff / Deil's kirnstaff

Some of these names apply to most spurges, which are slightly reminiscent in form of churnstaves, for churning butter – the mention of the Devil references the poisonous and irritant sap. A selection of the modern Gaelic names are given too, but many are modern inventions, as some species are very rare or local, such as sea spurge, which is only found on the Solway Firth and a few spots on the Clyde coast.

ST. JOHN'S WORT
(*Hypericum* species)

ENGLISH: Aaron's beard; Jonet

GAELIC: *Achlasan Chaluim Chille*; *Allas Chaluim Chille* – glory or image of St. Columba; *Allas Mhoire / Allas Mhuire* – glory or image of Mary; *Allhabi*; *Beachnuadh boireann*; *Beachnuadh boireonn*; *Caod* – to come; *Caod achlasen Chalum-chille* – the flower borne by St. Columba; *Caod aslachan Cholum chille*; *Caod-Chaluim-Chille* – St. Columba's armpit package; *Caora-caothaich*; *Eala bhuidhe / Ealbhuidhe* – golden-yellow in appearance; *Lus-an fhograidh* – plant of exile; *Lus-Chaluim-Chille* – St. Columba's plant; *Seud-Chaluim-Chille* – St. Columba's jewel

As the sheer number of names attests, the St. John's worts were extremely important, and indeed, appear almost revered as practically every name listed here, and many others throughout Europe, tie this plant to the saints or to the Virgin Mary herself. This is undoubtedly due to its use as an antidepressant – although the action of the plant is not well understood even today, it was long-interpreted as a blessed plant that could chase away demons – one interpretation of depression and other psychiatric illnesses.

STITCHWORTS
(*Stellaria* species)

ENGLISH: Break-bones; Snap-stalks – specifically Greater stitchwort (*Stellaria holostea*)

GAELIC: *Fiodh na nathrach*; *Flidh na nathrach*; *Tuirseach / Tursarain / Tursarainin / Tursarranin* – dejected neglected

The English common names for the slender, silvery woodland species refer to its brittle stems, a feature of several other species in the genus. The Gaelic names are more general for stitchworts.

STONECROP, BITING
(*Sedum acre*)

ENGLISH: Lover's links

GAELIC: *Glas lann / Glas lean* – a green spot, apparently from *leana* = meadow; *Gràbhan nan Clach / Grafan nan clach / Gràfan nan Clach* – stone pickaxe or stone mattock from the plant's apparent ability to grow from stone, from *grabhan* = a mattock and *clach* = a stone

This little plant looks a like a chain of succulent leaves and can grow in inhospitable, stony ground.

SUGAR WRACK OR SUGAR KELP
(*Saccharina latissima*)

ENGLISH: Poor man's weather glass; Sea belt

GAELIC: *Milearach*; *Smeartan* – a smear, or greasy

SCOTS: Sweet sea-tangle

This broad-fronded, chunky brown seaweed has a tough frond, but is used even now as a stock for flavouring soups and stews, akin to Japanese kombu, which is closely related. This seaweed contains the sweet substance mannitol, which gives it the common English names.

SUNDEWS
(*Drosera* species)

GAELIC: *Dealt ruaidhe* – red-dew; *Driuchd-a'-mhonaidh* / *Druchdan-monaidh* – morning dew of the mountains; *Druchd-a'-mona*; *Druchd-a'-muine* – dew of the morning, or dew of the hill; *Gadmann*; *Gadmunn*; *Gealdraidh* / *Gealdruidh* – red dew; *Lus-an-earnaich*; *Lus na feàrnaich* – plant of the murrain

Round-leaved sundew (*Drosera rotundifolia*) is *Lus na feàrnaich* – plant of the shield, plant of the Alder or plant or the murrain; *Lus na-fearna-guirme* – the blueish shield or bluish Alder; *Ros-an-t-soluis* – rose of the sun

These carnivorous little plants are widespread in peaty, boggy soils where nutrients are hard to come by. Round-leaved sundew (*Drosera rotundifolia*) is more common than the other species in Scotland and is the one with references to shields in the names, but most of the other's names are seemingly interchangeable among the sundews as a whole. The murrain is a disease of cattle – sundews and other plants of boggy areas were erroneously given the blame for causing the disease, although it may be that they were used more as 'indicator species' of poor grazing land rather than causing the disease directly.

SWEET CICELY
(*Myrrhis odorata*)

GAELIC: *Mirr*; *Cos uisge* – scented water plant

SCOTS: Mirr (Braemar); Myrrh (Aberdeenshire); Sweet humlick (Berwickshire)

Sweet cicely was introduced to Scotland from mainland Europe probably over a millennium ago for growing in monastery gardens. It escaped and has become a part of our wider flora, growing in shady woodlands, mostly through the lowlands. The anise-scented plant was used as a flavouring and is popular with foragers today as well. As a member of the Umbellifer family, it looks slightly similar to hemlock (*Conium maculatum*) but is delicious rather than deadly.

SWEET GRASS, FLOATING
(*Glyceria fluitans*)

GAELIC: *Feur-uisge* – water-grass; *Millteach-uisge*; *Milsean uisge* – sweet water grass

SCOTS: Flote-grass

A robust aquatic grass with floating leaves, these names serve it well.

SWEET VERNAL GRASS
(*Anthoxanthum odoratum*)

GAELIC: *Borrach* – from *boradh*, scent or smell; *Borran*; *Mislean* – from *milis*, sweet, sugary or honeyed

A common grass in many open habitats, this early flowering species gives off a strong scent of coumarin – of the compounds responsible for the smell of freshly mown hay.

SYCAMORE
(*Acer pseudoplatanus*)

ENGLISH: Great maple; Plane tree; Scots Plane

GAELIC: *Craobh pleantrain* – from planetree; *Craobh shice*; *Fir-crann / Fir chrann*; *Plinntrinn*; *Sicamor*; *Sice*

SCOTS: Maiser; Maizie

The sycamore was introduced to Scotland from Europe probably in late mediaeval times and has established itself as a major component of lowland woodlands, supporting a huge range of invertebrates and other organisms – it is very much at home here. The plane part of the sycamore's names comes from its similarity to true plane trees (*Platanus*), which were introduced and are more prevalent in the south of Britain. The Scots names are more general for maples and derive from the wood used to make the shallow 'maser' style of drinking bowls, although this was also often lime (*Tilia*) and walnut (*Juglans*) species.

T to Z

T

TANSY

(Tanacetum vulgare), and Feverfew *(Tanacetum parthenium)*

GAELIC: *Meadh-duach /*
Meadh-duaich; *Frangalus*; *Ialthus*

SCOTS: Featherfooly;
Stinkin Tam / Stinkin Tammie

The names for these two fragrant
and feathery-leaved species
of the daisy family are largely
interchangeable.

TEASEL
(*Dipsacus fullonum*)

ENGLISH: Great white teasel; Venus's basins

GAELIC: *Leadan / Liodan –* a head of hair or fuller of cloth; *Leadan an Fhùcadair*; *Liadan an fhùcadair / Liodan-an-fhucadair –* the fuller of cloth; *Lus-an-fhucadair*

This stately biennial plant adds a touch of class to its typical habitat of roadside ditches. The flowerheads last long into winter and are a great source of seeds for goldfinches. Flowers are usually purple, but individuals with white flowers are common. Folklore holds that water gathered from the basin-like structure where the paired leaves join can be used as a beauty treatment, although it usually contains a bit of a soup of dead insects!

THISTLE
(*Cirsium* and *Carduus* species)

These names are fairly general across thistles, although several of the more distinct species have names particular to them, such as carline thistle (*Carlina vulgaris*) which is *cluaran oir* – golden thistle, or *foghnan-soilleir / fothannan-soilleir* – bright thistle. The soft-leaved melancholy thistle (*Cirsium heterophyllum*) is *cluas an Fhèidh* – deer's ear in Gaelic, and in Scots shares the names 'curly-head' or 'Carl doddie' with many similar purple-flowered, thistle-like plants such as knapweed (*Centaurea nigra*). Also like many of these species, the mass of fused flower stalks in the middle of the head was eaten as a snack – somewhat like artichoke hearts. They have a consistency like cheese, hence the name. The spear thistle (*Cirsium vulgare*) has the most individual names, so has a separate entry below.

ENGLISH: Cheese

GAELIC: *Cluaran* - thistle; *Diogan*; *Foghnan*; *Giogan*

SCOTS: Porr / Purr; Thirstle; Thrissel; Thrussel / Thrustle; Thustle; Tissel (Orkney); Tistle (Orkney, Shetland)

THISTLE, SPEAR
(*Cirsium vulgare*)

GAELIC: *Cluaran deilgheach* – prickly thistle; *An Deilgneach* – prickly; *Fothannan glas* (Colonsay); *Grualan* (Lochalsh)

SCOTS: Bur-thistle (Ayrshire); Burr thrissel; Scotch thissel

This is the largest native thistle, and one of the strongest contenders for Scotland's national plant, along with the introduced Mediterranean species cotton thistle (*Onopordon acanthium*).

THONG WEED
(*Himanthalia elongata*)

ENGLISH: Sea beans; Sea spaghetti; Sea thong

GAELIC: *Imleag / Iomlach / Iomleach*

SCOTS: Drew (Orkney)

This robust brown seaweed of the lower shore was used as a stock and thickener for soups and stews, especially mutton and lamb. The mushroom-shaped basal part was for this, while the longer strap, or thong-like upper parts were cut up and eaten like spaghetti. The bean-like crunchy consistency gave them the name 'sea beans'.

THRIFT
(*Armeria maritima*)

ENGLISH: Sea-daisy; Sea-thrift

GAELIC: *Barr-dearg* – red top; *Brisgean-traghad*; *Fiantanan* (South Uist, Eriskay); *Milsean-mara* – sweetie of the sea; *Neòinean cladaich* – beach daisy; *Tonn a' Chladaich* – beach wave

SCOTS: Arby (Orkney)

This cheerful little plant of saltmarshes and cliffs is not related to daisies, although they do look somewhat similar.

THYME
(*Thymus* species)

ENGLISH: Mother of thyme

GAELIC: *Lus an Rìgh* – King's plant; *Lus an tigh*; *Lus mhic righ Bhreatainn* – plant of the King of the Britons' son; *Lus na Macraidh*; *Meitheachan* (South Uist, Eriskay)

SCOTS: Tae-girse – tea-plant (Shetland)

These names apply to most of the thyme species, both garden and wild.

TORMENTIL
(*Potentilla erecta*)

ENGLISH: Blood-root; Ewe-daisy; Flesh-and-blood; Shepherd's knot (Berwickshire)

GAELIC: *Braonan nan con* – dog's bud; *Braonan-a'-mhadaidh ruaidh* (Colonsay); *Braonan-bachlaig* – bud of the shoot; *Braonan-fraoich* – bud of the heather; *Cairt Làir* – ground bark; *Cairt-leamhna / Cairt-leamhnach* (South Uist, Eriskay); *Cara-mhil-a'-choin* – possibly from *cara-mhill*, mandrake, so 'the dog's mandrake'; *Leamhnach / Leamhnachd* – to be followed; *Leamnhnach* – tormenting; *Leanartach / Leannartach* – to follow

SCOTS: Aert-Bark – earth-bark (Shetland); Eart-bart / Eartbar / Earth-barth – earth bark

Tormentil is a small plant of acid grasslands and heaths, widespread and common, so it was perhaps 'the follower' as it could be found anywhere, or maybe because its stems wander through the neighbouring vegetation, which is where the name tormentil is said to come from. In areas without trees its deep-red tuber was an important source of tannin for tanning leather in lieu of bark, hence the many variants on 'earth-bark'. The Gaelic mention of mandrake is perhaps a little tenuous, as *cara-mhill* is just as likely to relate to bitter vetch (*Lathyrus linifolius*), another useful tuberous plant found commonly beside tormentil.

TURNIP
(*Brassica rapa*)

GAELIC: *Neip / Neup*; *Neip fiadhain*; *Sneip*; *Tuimpe*

SCOTS: Neep; Rap (SW Scotland); Rorie; Taupin (Perthshire, NE Scotland); Tumshie; Turmit; Turneep

These names for the humble turnip, mostly derive ultimately from *rapus* or *napus*, the Latin for this plant and its close relative.

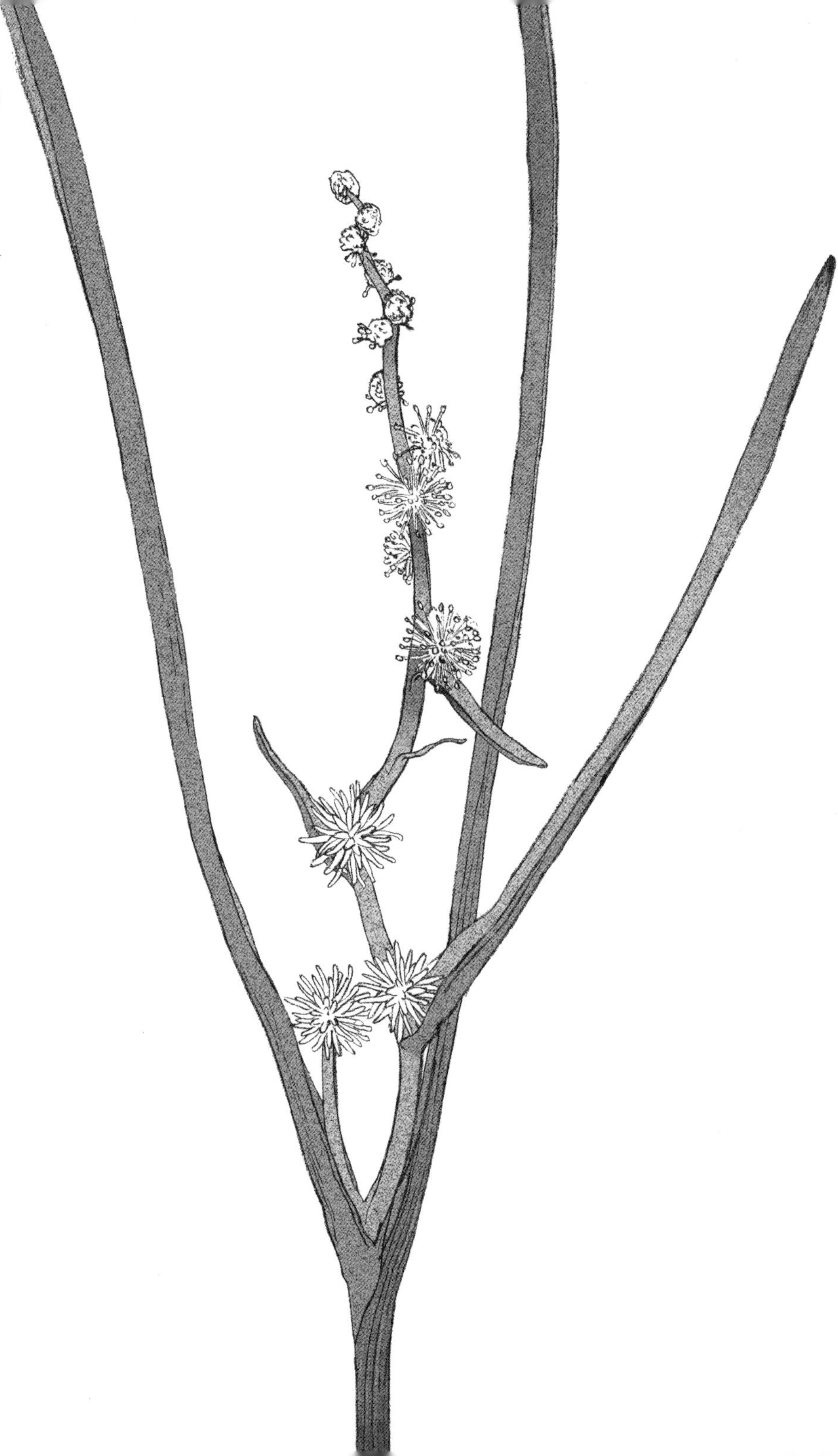

U

UNBRANCHED BUR-REED
(*Sparganium emersum*)

GAELIC: *Seasg / Seisg; Seisg madaidh / Seisg madraidh* – dog's sedge; *Seisg Rìgh Madaidh* – king dog's sedge

Most of these names have a 'sedge' element, but the dog references are suggested to come from its flowering time in July – the 'dog-days', although this may be a bit of a stretch, 'dog' names are often applied to smaller, or in this case rougher, more robust versions of plants.

V

VALERIAN
(*Valeriana officinalis* and other species)

ENGLISH: Great wild valerian

GAELIC: *Carthan curaidh* / *Carthan curaigh* – useful tall plant, or useful hero; *Lus-bileach* – leaf plant; *Lus na snathaid*; *Lus na tri bhilean* / *Lus-nan-tri-bilean* / *Tri-bhileach* / *Tribhileach* – three-leaved, -lipped or -fringed plant

SCOTS: Valairie

Valerian has long been an important medicinal plant, so is well known and has picked up a few names. Many of the Gaelic ones are a variant on three-leaved, which is a tenuous description of the leaf that splits into many more than three lobes. There may be some degree of confusion with other trefoils, such as bogbean (*Menyanthes trifoliata*), which shares many of these names, but this is unlikely – perhaps the three refers to the cymose flowerheads that split into three tufts.

Marsh valerian (*Valeriana dioica*) is *caoirin Lèana* – little berry of the marsh, referring to the fruits, but the alternative name, *carthan arraigh*, is more romantic, evoking the pinky-white flowers of summer as 'that which gleams in the marsh'.

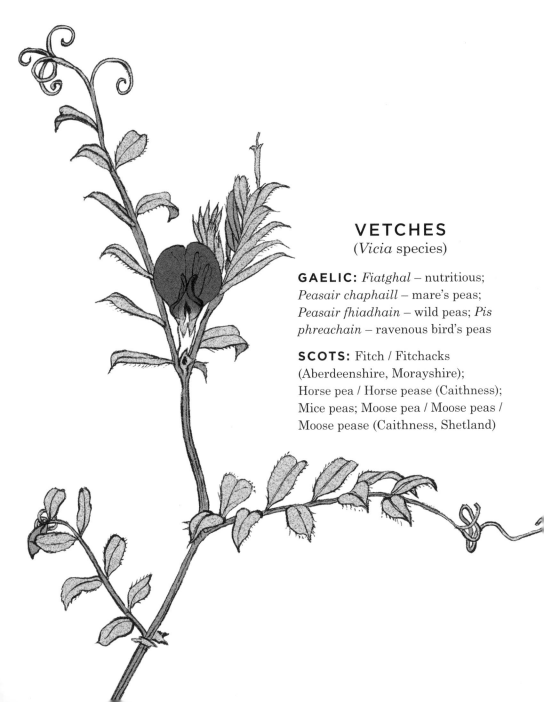

VETCHES
(*Vicia* species)

GAELIC: *Fiatghal* – nutritious;
Peasair chaphaill – mare's peas;
Peasair fhiadhain – wild peas; *Pis
phreachain* – ravenous bird's peas

SCOTS: Fitch / Fitchacks
(Aberdeenshire, Morayshire);
Horse pea / Horse pease (Caithness);
Mice peas; Moose pea / Moose peas /
Moose pease (Caithness, Shetland)

Vetches are a diverse group of legumes in the pea family, and effectively include the peas proper. The common vetch (*Vicia sativa*) is perhaps the most commonly referred to by the names given here, as it is widespread, especially near farms and towns, and a nutritious favourite of horses. Bush vetch (*V. sepium*) is a similar robust and common species, so shares some of these names, although its standard Gaelic name is a literal translation, *peasair nam preas* – 'pea of the bush'. The same is true of the little spring vetch, *vicia lathyroides – peasair an earraich,* and the rarer wood vetch (*Vicia sylvatica*) *peasair coile* – 'wood pea' in Gaelic. Similarly, the exceedingly rare wood bitter vetch (*Vicia orobus*) is *peasair searbh* or *peasair shearbh* – meaning bitter pea, although it drops the wood element. For the much-famed 'true' bitter vetch (*Lathyrus linifolius*), please see the separate entry. Both the hairy tare (*Vicia hirsuta*) and tufted vetch (*Vicia cracca*) are sufficiently striking as to have garnered more names as well, so there are separate entries for them too.

VETCH, BITTER
(*Lathyrus linifolius*)

ENGLISH: Heath-pea; Heath-vetch; Tuberous-rooted bitter vetchling

GAELIC: *Cairmeal* – enjoyable thing of the moss; *Cairt Leamhna*; *Caorrthanan*; *Cara-meilidh*; *Carmel*; *Carraicean*; *Carra-meille*; *Charmel / Charmelic*; *Corra-meille*; *Knaphard*; *Peasair-tuilbh*

SCOTS: Caperoiles; Carameil; Carmele; Carmylie; Cormeille; Corra-meile; Gnapperts; Gowk's gilly-flower – shared with other pink-flowered plants flowering in May; Heather-pease; Knapperts; Napple

This remarkable little plant had a huge reputation in recent centuries. The tubers were dug up and eaten to suppress the appetite, and apparently imbue the eater with energy. It was also a valued flavouring for whisky and other spirits. Through the 18th and 19th centuries, this plant's reputation grew, although it was never brought into widespread use or cultivation. The names do appear somewhat muddled between Scots and Gaelic in particular, and there may be considerable crossover and misrecording in the names. In any case, the large number of names is testimony to its importance. The -meal, -mel, -meille, and similar elements may relate to honey, an allusion to the sweet flavour of the tubers. However, recent research suggests it may not be as innocuous as was once thought, and pending further investigations, it should not be eaten.

VETCH, TUFTED
(*Vicia cracca*)

GAELIC: *Caornan* (Colonsay);
Peasair nan Luch – mice peas;
Peasair-luchag – little mouse peas;
Peasair-luch-na-coille – wood
mouse peas; *Pesair-radain* –
rat's peas

SCOTS: Blue Girse
(Shetland); Cat peas; Fitchacks
(Aberdeenshire); Wild fetches;
Wild Tare

A cheerful little vetch of mid and
late summer, producing copious
small pods from its tuft of purple
flowers. Although the fruits are
small, 'mouse peas' might better
describe the related hairy vetchling
(*Ervum hirsutum*), whose pods
look even more like a plump
little mouse.

VINE, GRAPE
(*Vitis vinifera*)

GAELIC: *Crann-fiona* / *Crann fionan* / *Craobh-fhiona* – wine tree, the vine; *Dearc-an-fhiona* / *Fion-chaor* / *Fion-dearcag* / *Fion-dhearc* – wine berry, the grape

SCOTS: Wyne; Wynne; Vin

Although vines were usually only grown under cover in Scotland, wine has always been popular, and vines are fundamental motifs through Biblical tradition, so were well-known and correspondingly well-named.

VIOLETS
(*Viola* species)

Some of the names for several species of violets in Scotland are shared across them all, as the species are fairly similar. In Gaelic, *cuach*, a bowl, is a general term for them, often qualified with another word according to the species. The idea of them as a drinking bowl is also found in their Scots names, while Gaelic sometimes picks up on the spur at the base of the flower, likening it to a cuckoo's toe or claw. Names for particular species are discussed below:

HEATH DOG VIOLET
(*Viola canina*)

GAELIC: *Dàil-chuach* – field bowl; *Fanaidse / Fanaigse* – possibly weak or fragile; *Sàil-chuach* – apparently Cuckoo's heel

SWEET **VIOLET**
(*Viola odorata*)

ENGLISH: Love-idleness

GAELIC: *Ail-chuach*; *Fail chuach* / *Fail cuaich* – scented bowl (South Uist, Eriskay); *Brog-na-cuthaig*

SCOTS: Blaver; Cogie – drinking cup; Quaich – drinking bowl, from Gaelic *chuach*

WILD PANSY
(*Viola tricolor*)

ENGLISH: Heartsease

GAELIC: *Brog-na-cubhaige* – cuckoo's shoe; *Fluran-cluigeanach, Am* / *Pluran-cluigeannach, Am* – little clustered flower; *Goirmean-searradh* / *Goirmin-an-searradh* – blue bottle; *Luibh chridhe* – heart-herb, heartsease; *Spog na cubhaig* – cuckoo's claw

SCOTS: Pancy / pansé / pauncé / pawnsy / pensée; Vylet

WATERCRESS
(*Nasturtium officinale*)

ENGLISH: Lily

GAELIC: *Biolar / Biolur* –
cress dainty or causes the nose to
smart; *Biolar Moire* – Mary's cress;
Biolair-uaine – green cress;
Biorar – from *bior* = water and
feur = grass; *Dobhar-lus / Durlus* –
water plant; *Dubhar*; *Dubhrach*;
Treabhach

SCOTS: Geraflouer; Gerofle;
Kerses – from Anglo-Saxon *Caerse* =
cress; Lillie; Wall-kerses; Well-
girse; Well-karse; Wild skirret

An important salad herb and
savoury flavouring, watercress was
and still is popular. The reference to
Mary in *Biolar Moire* may reference
the pure white, four-petalled flower
in a crucifix formation, or perhaps
its association with wells, which
were often considered sacred to
Christ's mother.

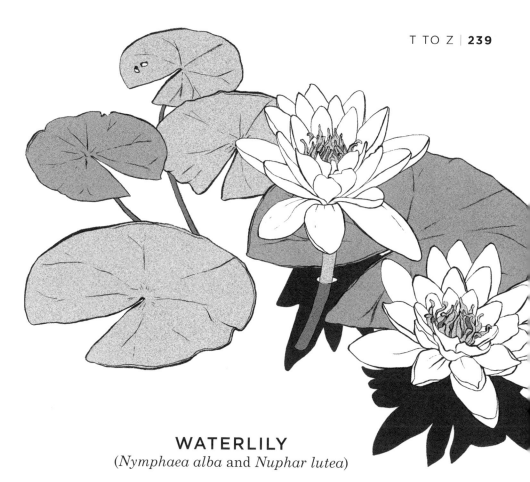

WATERLILY
(*Nymphaea alba* and *Nuphar lutea*)

SCOTS: Bobbins – bundles; Cambie leaf (N. Scotland); Lily-can (Fife, Perthshire)

GAELIC: *Bileag-bhaite*; *Bior-ros*; *Cairt-locha*; *Cuirinnein*; *Duilleag bhan* – white leaf; *Duilleag-bhàite bhan* – drowned white leaf; *Gucag bhaite / Gucagan-baite* – the water cup(s); *Lili bhan* – white lily; *Rabhagach* – warning; *Ruaimleadh* – warning beacon (Colonsay)

The names mentioning white (*bhan*) refer to the white waterlily (*Nymphaea alba*), while the yellow waterlily (*Nuphar lutea*) is: *duileag-bhàite bhuidhe* – yellow drowned leaf; *duilleag-bhuidhe* – yellow-leaf and *lili-bhuidhe-an-uisge*. Cambie is recorded in Jamieson's *Dictionary of Scots* (1808), although the derivation is unknown. The most evocative names are perhaps the Gaelic ones portraying the plants as a warning to the unwary in danger of drowning.

WRACKS
(*Ascophyllum nodosum* and *Fucus* species)

ENGLISH: Bell-weed; Dyer's wrack; Kelp-Wrack; Lady-wrack; Popweed; Pig-weed; Rock weed; Red wrack

GAELIC: *Feamainn* – apparently from 'tail' or 'rump', but this term is used for seaweeds in general; *Grob / Grobach* – to dig or grub; *Lianaich*; *Prablach / Propach* – tangled; *Trailleach*

SCOTS: Bell-ware; Black tang; Kelp-ware; Paddy tang (Orkney), Sea-ware, Vraic; Yellow-Tang

The wracks are chunky brown seaweeds and some of the names are interchangeable among the common species of *fucus*, as well as the egg-wrack (*Ascophyllum nodosum*). This latter species, along with bladderwrack (*Fucus vesiculosus*) have air bladders to help the fronds float, so these are the 'popweeds'. Several of these seaweeds change colour late in the season – becoming yellowish or red-orange from black-brown earlier in the spring and summer. Hence many of the colour-change names. Knotted wrack tends to become yellow, but this is inconsistent and depends on conditions, so it is unlikely that the names are consistently applied to a particular scientific species in different areas. All of them are used as fertiliser and were burned for kelp-ash in the 18th and 19th centuries.

WRACK, SERRATED
(*Fucus serratus*)

ENGLISH: Saw-wrack; toothed wrack; wrack

GAELIC: *Aon-chasach* – one-stemmed; *Buidheagach*; *Feamiainn dubh* – black seaweed or wrack; *Ramasg*; *Slaodach*

SCOTS: Prickly tang

Serrated wrack is a robust seaweed from low on the shore, distinctive for the softly toothed margin to the frond.

WHEAT
(*Triticum* species and cultivated varieties)

ENGLISH: Corn; Gray corn;
Shot blade

GAELIC: *Currachd an righ*;
Fasanach; *Fideag*

SCOTS: Aicher; Icker; White
(NE Scotland)

Wheat and its many products have a host of names, but only a selection are given here. In Scotland, both barley (*Hordeum* species) and oats (*Avena sativa*) have been of equal or even greater importance through various times and regions. Currently much of the cereal production is barley for the whisky and brewing industries.

WILLOWHERB
(*Chamerion angustifolium* and *Epilobium* species)

GAELIC: *Eilig* (Glenlyon);
Seileachan Frangach –
French willow

SCOTS: French Saugh –
French willow

These names all relate to
rosebay willowherb (*Chamerion
angustifolium*), a tall herb of
weedy communities that is named
for its slender, willow-like leaves,
although it is unrelated to true
willows. The 'French' element of
the names in Gaelic and Scots
may refer either to the elegant
form and striking pink-petalled
flowers, or to its unclear origin
from 'foreign shores'. Indeed, the
origin of rosebay willowherb is
poorly understood.

WILLOW
(*Salix* species)

GAELIC: *Saileog / Sal*; *Seileach*; *Suil*; *Sùileag*

SCOTS: Sauch; Sauch buss – willow bush; Sauch tree; Sauch wan / Sauch wand – willow wand or switch; Sauch-willie; Scob / Scub; Scrog Widdie; Willie

Willows share several names, and a few of the more useful or distinct have individual names as well, listed below:

WILLOW, GOAT
(*Salix caprea*)

ENGLISH: Great sallow; Common sallow

GAELIC: *Crann-seilich*; *Craobh-sheilich*; *Dubh-sheileach*; *Geal-sheileach / Seileach-geal* – perhaps white willow (*Salix alba*); *Sùileag* – a general name for willows more recently applied to sallow

SCOTS: Saugh; Saugh tree

A shrubby or small tree species with broad, elliptic leaves.

WILLOW, OSIER
(*Salix viminalis*)

ENGLISH: Cooper's willow

GAELIC: *Bun*; *Bunnsach*;
Bunsach; *Bunsag* – stump or
stock from the coppiced stools;
Fineamhuin – long twig;
Gall sheileach – foreign willow;
Maothan; *Saileach uisge* / *Seileach-
uisge* – water willow (Colonsay)

SCOTS: Osare

Osier is one of the most commonly
used species for coppicing to
produce withies – the long,
flexible wands used in basketry,
fence-making and for a host of
other purposes.

WILLOW, WHITE
(*Salix alba*)

GAELIC: *Seileach Bàn* –
white willow; *Crann-seilich* /
Craobh-sheilich – willow tree;
Geal-sheileach

A large species with distinctly
white undersides to the leaves.

WOOD ANEMONE
(*Anemone nemorosa*)

ENGLISH: Windflower

GAELIC: *Flùr na gaoithe*;
Plur na gaoithe

SCOTS: Darn grass;
Wild jessamine – wild jasmine
(Dumfriesshire)

'Windflower' and *flùr na gaoithe* are fairly close renditions of the Greek origin – 'anemo-' is wind or breeze and is a beautifully evocative name for this cheerful early spring plant of woodlands and nearby heaths. In stark contrast, 'darn' can mean faeces in Scots, which is perhaps a bit less romantic but refers to a gastric disease of livestock caused when they eat the plants. Perhaps the most intriguing thing is the very few, and mostly consistent, names for the plant. It wasn't particularly used in the past, but it is a striking and easily identified species. Perhaps in a similar way to other plants widely found in areas where Indo-European languages are found, its name was given a millennia ago, and the meaning has stuck even through translation into the languages within the bigger language family.

WOOD AVENS
(*Geum urbanum*)

ENGLISH: Herb Bennet

GAELIC: *Benedin*; *Machall coille* –
flower of the wood; *Traithnin*

This common, somewhat weedy plant is a 'herba benedicta', a blessed herb. It was used in medicine, as well as for flavouring, particularly the rootstock, which has a fragrance of cloves.

WOOD SORREL
(Oxalis acetosella)

ENGLISH: Cuckoo sorrel;
Cuckoo's meat; Lady's clover;
Sour clover (Berwickshire)

GAELIC: *Biadh nan coinean*;
Samh

SCOTS: Gowk's meat (N Scotland)

This delicate little woodland plant
is quite clover like with soft trefoil
leaves, although the flower is very
different. Popular with foragers
past and present, its sour, sorrel-
like taste is distinctive. Like many
other plants named for the cuckoo,
it does tend to flower around May-
time, when the cuckoo can be heard
calling, although cuckoo has the
double meaning of fool.

WOODRUFF
(Galium odoratum)

GAELIC: *Gairgean / Geirgein*;
Lus a' Chaitheamh – plant for
tuberculosis, or consumption
(South Uist, Eriskay); *Lus molach* –
hairy plant

SCOTS: Kirst-weed; Sweet-grass
(Berwickshire), White-flowered
woodroof; Witherips; Woodrep /
Woodrip

This dainty little woodland species
has a scent of fresh-mown hay due
to the compound coumarin. The
Scots names are almost playful in
their variants. However, the Gaelic
lus molach is a little more subtle –
although the plant is generally
hairless, it perhaps refers to the
tufted appearance of a patch of the
plants in dappled woodland sun.

WOUNDWORTS
(*Stachys* species)

ENGLISH: Wood betony –
for *Stachys sylvatica*

GAELIC: *Biatas*; *Glasair coille* –
green one of the wood; *Lus bheathag* –
life plant; *Lus nan scorr / Lus nan
Sgor* – wound wort; *Brisgean-nan-
caorach* (Colonsay); *Cuislean-gun-
dorainn*; *Cuislean-gun-doruinn*

SCOTS: Cockhead (Lanarkshire);
Hound's tongue (Morayshire);
Maskert; Swine arnit / Swinen
arnit – earth-nut (Banffshire);
Swine's Beads (Shetland);
Swine's maskert; Swines Murricks
(Shetland) – pig's bulbs or tubers

Most of the Scots names seem to
be applied to Marsh woundwort
(*stachys palustris*) but a few are
shared with other plants, such
as Hound's tongue, also used for
species of *cynoglossum*, a member
of the borage family, or Swine's
beads, used for several plants with
underground tubers favoured by
pigs. It may be that there is some
error in recording here. As both
English and Gaelic names suggest,
these species were important
styptics or vulneraries used in
treating wounds.

Y

YARROW
(*Achillea millefolium*)

ENGLISH: Hundred-leaved grass (Berwickshire); Milfoil; Thousand-leaf clover (Berwickshire); Wild pepper (Berwickshire)

GAELIC: *Athair-thalmhainn* – the earth father or ground father; *Barr-thalmhainn*; *Cair-thalamhainn*; *Cathair-lair*; *Cathair-thalanda*; *Cathair-thalmhainn* – ground chair; *Earr-thal-mainn* – tail of the earth; *Earr-thalmhainn* – that which clothes the ground; *Lus na fala* (Skye) / *Lus na fola* – blood plant; *Lus-an-t-Sleisneach* – large-thighed plant; *Lus-chosgadh-na-fola* – plant that staunches bleeding

SCOTS: Doggie's brose; Meal-and-folie (Shetland); Melancholy (Shetland); Moleery-tea; Stanch-girs (Caithness); Yarra

The names of this common grassland plant are wonderfully varied – many relate to its use as a dressing to staunch the flow of blood – a tradition that goes back to Achilles, hence even the taxonomic Latin name speaks of the same use. The plant's appearance, with its intricately feathery leaves gives rise to other names, while its resistance to trampling makes it seem to spring direct from even the most packed and trodden turf, giving the references to earth and ground in the names.

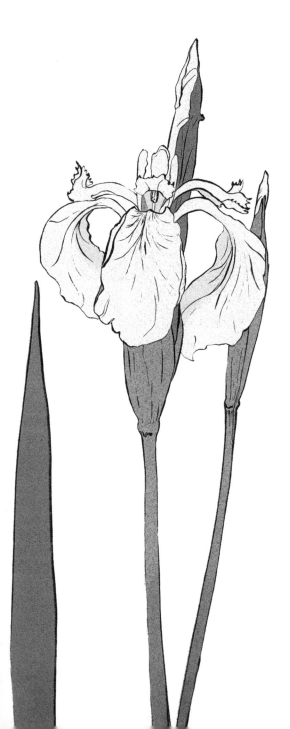

YELLOW FLAG IRIS
(*Iris pseudacorus*)

ENGLISH: Flag; Fleur-de-lys; Wild Iris

GAELIC: *Bior-bhogha* – sharp-bow, although unlikely derivation; *Bogha-froise*; *Bogha-uisge* – rainbow; *Sealasdair* – sunlight or rainbow plant; *Seileasdair* / *Seileasdear* / *Seilisdear* / *Seilisdeir* / *Siolastar*

SCOTS: Cheeper / Cheiper / Cheper (Roxburghshire, Lothian); Dug's lug – dog's ear (Shetland); Saggon (Lanarkshire); Seg / Segg – sedge; Seggan (Argyll, Bute, Ayrshire) / Seggen – sedges; Water-skegg

Scotland's only native *Iris* species, this large, yellow-flowered wetland plant is common in dense stands, often near the sea, especially in the west. The Gaelic names recall the near Europe-wide names derived from its place in Greek myth, where Iris is the goddess of rainbows. Various interpretations have been overlaid since, with the rainbow-related names in Gaelic said to relate to its widespread use as a dye – from dark browns and blacks, yellows through to greens. As is strikingly common, the Scots names are more prosaic. Cheepers and variants refer to its value as an impromptu musical instrument – as with various grasses, the leaf can be held between the thumbs and used as a reed to make a strident cheeping noise. Although it is clearly not a sedge in the botanical sense, it has adopted the general name Segg, and variants, like many other wetland monocots (with slender leaves).

YELLOWRATTLE
(*Rhinanthus minor*)

GAELIC: *Bainne nan luch*
(South Uist, Eriskay); *Bodach nan*
claigeann / Bodach-nan-claigionn –
old man with the skulls; *Modalan-*
buidhe / Modhalan buidhe –
the little or modest yellow one

SCOTS: Doggins; Dog's pennies
(Shetland); Dog's siller; Gowk's
shillings / Gowk's siller – fool's or
cuckoo's shillings (Roxburghshire)

Yellowrattle is a widespread
grassland plant which is now
extensively planted for its ability to
suppress robust grasses, encouraging
other, more showy flowering plants,
as it is parasitic on the grass
species. This remarkable feature
may not really have been noticed
as significant, as the idea does not
appear in any of the names, rather
it is the large, disc-shape seeds that
sit loosely in the dried fruits that
give it many of its names. Plucked
and shaken you can hear these
seeds rattling in the fruit like silver
pennies in a fat purse. The best
name, however, has to be the Gaelic
bodach nan claigeann – the inflated
fruits do indeed look just like old,
weathered skulls.

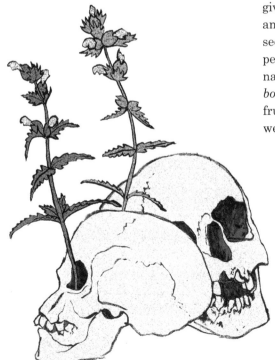

YEW
(*Taxus baccata*)

GAELIC: *Crann-iubhair* / *Craobh-iubhair* – yew tree or wood from the yew; *Dearc-an-iubhair* – yew berry; **Iogh**; *Ioghar*; *Ioua*; *Iubhar*; *Iuthar*; *Iughar*; *Sinnsior* / *Sinsior* – ancient; *Togh*; *Tuagh* – obsolete name for a bow, now a hatchet or axe

SCOTS: Ewe

Although yew is not thought to be native to Scotland, the truly ancient plants found in significant religious sites suggest it has long held an important place in belief since pre-Christian times. Indeed, Yew is one of the fundamental trees across Indo-European languages, and the tales of derivation for its names are many and varied. In Gaelic, the name is supposedly derived from *iùi*, an arrow, as it was used for the finest bows, and arrows were poisoned with a dangerous cocktail including Yew – it is one of the most poisonous plants in our flora. However, the likeness to similar names throughout wider northern Europe is evident, so it likely has an even earlier derivation. This is a similar pattern to the Greek 'taxus' itself, from which we derive 'toxic' – 'toxes' meant archer in classical Greek. These concepts of the plant, bows and poisoned arrows are intricately bound up, and it is a good case of which came first, the chicken or the egg. In Scots, the name is simply a derivation of the same *iùi*, or yew.

Yew represents the letter I as *Iogh* in the Gaelic alphabet of tree names.

Bibliography

This is by no means a complete listing for all the sources consulted for this book but is hopefully a useful pointer to some of the other collated works and resources available.

BOOKS

BARKER, A., *Remembered Remedies: Scottish Traditional Plant Lore*, Birlinn, Edinburgh, 2011

BEITH, M., *Healing Threads: Traditional Medicines of the Highlands and Islands*, Birlinn, Edinburgh, 2004

CAMERON, J., *Gaelic Names of Plants (Scottish and Irish)*, William Blackwood and Sons, Edinburgh, 1883

CARMICHAEL, A., *Carmina Gadelica Ortha Nan Gaidheal*: Vols I–V., Oliver and Boyd, Edinburgh, 1928

CLARK, J.W. AND MACDONALD, I., *Ainmean Gaidhlig Lusan: Gaelic Names of Plants*, J.W. Clark, North Ballachulish, 1999

CLYNE, D., *Gaelic names for flowers and plants*, Cruisgean, Furnace, 1989

DARWIN, T., *The Scots Herbal: Plant Lore of Scotland*, Mercat Press, Edinburgh, 1996

DONALDSON, D., *Supplement to Jamieson's Scottish Dictionary*, Alexander Gardner, Paisley, 1887

DWELLY, E., *Faclair Gaidhlig Gu Beurla Le Dealbhan: Dwelly's Illustrated Gaelic to English Dictionary*, Gairm Publications, Glasgow, 2001

GARVIE, E.I., *Gaelic Names of Plants, Fungi and Animals*, Clò Ostaig, Slèite, 1999

GRANT, I.F., *Highland Folk Ways*, Birlinn, Edinburgh, 1995

GRIGSON, G., *The Englishman's Flora*, Phoenix House, London, 1987

JAMIESON, J., *An Etymological Dictionary of the Scottish Language*, University Press, Edinburgh, 1808

LIGHTFOOT, J., *Flora Scotica,* B. White, London, 1777

MABEY, R., *Flora Britannica,* Chatto & Windus, London, 1996

MACBAIN, A., *An Etymological Dictionary of the Gaelic Language,* Gairm Publications, Glasgow, 1982

MACFARLANE, A., *Gaelic Plant Names: Study of their Uses and Lore,* Gaelic Society of Inverness, Inverness, 1924

MCNEILL, M.F., *The Silver Bough,* William Maclellan, Glasgow, 1957

MILLIKEN, W. AND BRIDGEWATER, S., *Flora Celtica: Plants and People in Scotland,* Birlinn, Edinburgh, 2013

PANKHURST, R.J. AND MULLIN, J.M., *Flora of the Outer Hebrides,* Natural History Museum Publications, London, 1991

ROBERTSON, D., *Bho Bheul an Eòin / From the Bird's Mouth,* Woodlands Studios, Fife, 2022

ROBINSON, M., *Concise Scots Dictionary,* Polygon, Edinburgh, 1999

THOMSON, A., *A Scots Dictionary of Nature,* Saraband, Glasgow, 2019

WOOD, J., *Annals of the Andersonian Naturalists' Society,* Allan & Ferguson, Glasgow, 1893

WEBSITES

Botanical Society of Britain and Ireland, Biological Records Centre, UK Centre for Ecology and Hydrology, Joint Nature Conservation Committee, *Online Atlas of the British and Irish Flora,* https://plantatlas.brc.ac.uk (accessed May 2022)

Dictionaries of the Scots Language/ *Dictionars o the Scots Leid,* https://dsl.ac.uk (accessed May 2022)

Acknowledgements

Profound gratitude to Roger West for his immense contribution to the names database and to Alan Elliott and Matt Elliot for similarly valuable inputs. Thanks are also due to the many dedicated and wonderful colleagues, students and volunteers of the Royal Botanic Garden Edinburgh for your support and patience while compiling this book – especially those in the publications and education teams.